COOKING FOR TWO

by
Jean Paré

companyscoming.com
visit our ↑ website

Dedication

Just for two . . . me and you!

Cover Photo

Tablecloth Courtesy Of:
Chintz & Company

China Glasses, Cutlery And Linens Courtesy Of:
Eaton's China Dept.

COOKING FOR TWO

Copyright © Company's Coming Publishing Limited
All Rights Reserved

Eighth Printing February 2004

Canadian Cataloguing in Publication Data

Paré, Jean
Cooking for two

Issued also in French under title: La cuisine pour deux
Includes index.
ISBN 1-895455-27-8

1. Cookery for two. 2. Cookery. I. Title.
II. Series: Paré, Jean, Company's coming series

TX652.P37 1997   641.5'61   C97-018570-7

Published and Distributed by
Company's Coming Publishing Limited
2311 – 96 Street
Edmonton, Alberta, Canada T6N 1G3
www.companyscoming.com

**Published Simultaneously in
Canada and the United States of America**

Printed In Canada

Company's Coming Cookbook Series

Original Series

- Softcover, 160 pages
- 6" x 9" (15 cm x 23 cm) format
- Lay-flat binding
- Full colour photos
- Nutrition information

Quick & easy recipes, everyday ingredients!

Greatest Hits Series

- Softcover, 106 & 124 pages
- 8" x 9 9/16" (20 cm x 24 cm) format
- Paperback binding
- Full colour photos
- Nutrition information

Lifestyle Series

- Softcover, 160 pages
- 8" x 10" (20 cm x 25 cm) format
- Paperback & spiral binding
- Full colour photos
- Nutrition information

Most Loved Series

- Hardcover, 128 pages
- 8 3/4" x 8 3/4" (22 cm x 22 cm) format
- Full colour throughout
- Nutrition information

Special Occasion Series

- Hardcover & softcover, 192 pages
- 8 1/2" x 11" (22 cm x 28 cm) format
- Durable sewn binding
- Full colour throughout
- Nutrition information

See page 157 for a complete listing of cookbooks or visit www.companyscoming.com

table of Contents

the Jean Paré story

Jean Paré grew up understanding that the combination of family, friends and home cooking is the essence of a good life. From her mother she learned to appreciate good cooking, while her father praised even her earliest attempts. When she left home she took with her many acquired family recipes, her love of cooking and her intriguing desire to read recipe books like novels!

In 1963, when her four children had all reached school age, Jean volunteered to cater to the 50th anniversary of the Vermilion School of Agriculture, now Lakeland College. Working out of her home, Jean prepared a dinner for over 1000 people which launched a flourishing catering operation that continued for over eighteen years. During that time she was provided with countless opportunities to test new ideas with immediate feedback—resulting in empty plates and contented customers! Whether preparing cocktail sandwiches for a house party or serving a hot meal for 1500 people, Jean Paré earned a reputation for good food, courteous service and reasonable prices.

"Why don't you write a cookbook?" Time and again, as requests for her recipes mounted, Jean was asked that question. Jean's response was to team up with her son, Grant Lovig, in the fall of 1980 to form Company's Coming Publishing Limited. April 14, 1981, marked the debut of "150 DELICIOUS SQUARES", the first Company's Coming cookbook in what soon would become Canada's most popular cookbook series.

Jean Paré's operation has grown steadily from the early days of working out of a spare bedroom in her home. Full-time staff includes marketing personnel located in major cities across Canada. Home Office is based in Edmonton, Alberta in a modern building constructed specially for the company.

Today the company distributes throughout Canada and the United States in addition to numerous overseas markets, all under the guidance of Jean's daughter, Gail Lovig. Best-sellers many times over, Company's Coming cookbooks are published in English and French, plus a Spanish-language edition is available in Mexico. Familiar and trusted in home kitchens the world over, Company's Coming cookbooks are offered in a variety of formats, including the original softcover series.

Jean Paré's approach to cooking has always called for quick and easy recipes using everyday ingredients. Even when travelling, she is constantly on the lookout for new ideas to share with her readers. At home, she can usually be found researching and writing recipes, or working in the company's test kitchen. Jean continues to gain new supporters by adhering to what she calls "the golden rule of cooking": never share a recipe you wouldn't use yourself. It's an approach that works—*millions of times over!*

Foreword

There are certain to be many times in your life where you will find yourself cooking for two. As challenging as it may be to create large meals for family and friends, it can be just as demanding to prepare suitably-sized portions for two people. This book is the answer.

Some of the recipes in this cookbook call for less common cooking pan sizes. If you have trouble finding the specific size stated, you may find it among the wide variety of foil pans available. A small, 7 inch (17.5 cm) springform pan is handy to have around, but you can also improvise by lining the same size casserole dish with foil. You may also find a 6 cup muffin pan a useful purchase. It is recommended that you try to use the pan sizes indicated in the recipe. As well, some recipes use 1/2 portions of prepackaged foods. Unused portions of cake mix or onion soup mix can be stored in an airtight bag or container. Extra quantities of canned soup should be placed in an airtight plastic container and refrigerated or frozen for future use.

A nutrition analysis accompanies each recipe. Where an ingredient reads "sprinkle", "optional" or "just a pinch", it is not included as part of the nutritional information. The analysis uses 2% milk unless otherwise specified and if more than one ingredient is listed (such as "butter or hard margarine") then the first ingredient has been analyzed.

With all the choices this book has to offer, you will have fun deciding on what to make first! Sauced Salmon, page 81 or Cornish Hen For Two, page 75 is a great way to start. Fried Chicken, page 87 lends a whimsical touch of nostalgia while Shrimp Strata, page 104 is simply divine. Complete your meal with worry-free desserts like Frozen Peach Dessert, page 60 or Frosty Friday, page 63.

For anyone who has ever struggled to find recipes that make smaller portions, Cooking For Two is the perfect solution!

Jean Paré

Each recipe has been analyzed using the most up-to-date version of the Canadian Nutrient File from Health Canada, which is based on the United States Department of Agriculture (USDA) Nutrient Data Base. If more than one ingredient is listed (such as "hard margarine or butter"), or a range is given (1 – 2 tsp., 5 – 10 mL) then the first ingredient or amount is used in the analysis. Where an ingredient reads "sprinkle," "optional," or "for garnish," it is not included as part of the nutrition information. Milk, unless stated otherwise, is 1% and cooking oil, unless stated otherwise, is canola.

Margaret Ng, B.Sc. (Hon), M.A.
Registered Dietitian

CUCUMBER BITES

Quick and easy. You may want to double the recipe to allow more servings.

Cream cheese (2 tbsp., 30 mL)	1 oz.	28 g
Seasoned salt	$^1/_8$ tsp.	0.5 mL
Lemon juice, fresh or bottled	$^1/_8$ tsp.	0.5 mL
Round crackers	6	6
Cucumber slices, scored (see Note)	6	6
Pimiento slivers	6	6

Mash cream cheese, seasoned salt and lemon juice together on saucer.

Spread over crackers using 1 tsp. (5 mL) each. Top with cucumber slices.

Garnish each with pimiento sliver. Makes 6.

1 appetizer contains: 35 Calories (145 kJ); 22 g Fat; 1 g Protein; 48 mg Sodium

Note: To score cucumber, run tines of fork down sides of cucumber before slicing.

SHRIMP MOUSSE

Enjoy this snack for several evenings.

Envelope unflavored gelatin	1 x $^1/_4$ oz.	1 x 7 g
Water	$^1/_4$ cup	60 mL
Cream cheese, softened	4 oz.	125 g
Condensed tomato soup	$^1/_2$ x 10 oz.	$^1/_2$ x 284 mL
Salad dressing (or mayonnaise)	$^1/_3$ cup	75 mL
Finely chopped celery	$^1/_4$ cup	60 mL
Finely chopped green pepper	2 tbsp.	30 mL
Dry onion flakes	1 tsp.	5 mL
Lemon juice, fresh or bottled	1 tsp.	5 mL
Worcestershire sauce	1 tsp.	5 mL
Dill weed	$^1/_4$ tsp.	1 mL
Cooked shrimp, shredded or mashed	$^1/_2$ cup	125 mL
Crackers or tiny bread slices		

(continued on next page)

Sprinkle gelatin over water in small saucepan. Let stand 1 minute. Heat and stir to dissolve.

Beat cream cheese with soup and salad dressing in small bowl. Add gelatin mixture. Beat.

Add next 6 ingredients. Stir.

Add shrimp. Stir. Turn into 2 cup (500 mL) mold. Chill in refrigerator until set.

Unmold mousse onto serving plate. Serve with crackers and/or tiny bread slices. Makes 2 cups (500 mL).

¼ cup (60 mL) contains: 132 Calories (554 kJ); 10.9 g Fat; 4 g Protein; 273 mg Sodium

Pictured on page 17.

CRAB GEMS

This makes a good appetizer meal. May be used as open-faced sandwiches also.

Canned crabmeat, drained (or 1 cup, 250 mL fresh, cooked) membrane removed	4.2 oz.	120 g
Finely chopped green pepper	3 tbsp.	50 mL
Finely chopped onion	2 tbsp.	30 mL
Process sharp Cheddar cheese spread (such as Ingersoll)	½ cup	125 mL
Butter or hard margarine, softened	2 tbsp.	30 mL
Salad dressing (or mayonnaise)	1 tbsp	15 mL
Garlic salt	¼ tsp.	1 mL
Worcestershire sauce	¼ tsp.	1 mL
English muffins, halved	4	4

Stir crabmeat, green pepper and onion together in bowl.

Combine next 5 ingredients in separate bowl. Mix well. Add crabmeat mixture. Stir.

Spread over muffin halves. Cut each half into 4 pieces. Arrange on broiler pan. Broil for about 1½ minutes. These may be frozen before broiling and broiled without thawing first. Makes 32 appetizers (or 8 open-faced sandwiches).

1 appetizer contains: 42 Calories (176 kJ); 2 g Fat; 2 g Protein; 138 mg Sodium

Pictured on page 125.

STUFFED MUSHROOMS

Serve these hot as you relax on the deck.

Large mushrooms	6	6
Sausage meat	3 tbsp.	50 mL
Reserved chopped stems		
Cream cheese, softened (2 tbsp., 30 mL)	1 oz.	28 g
Dry bread crumbs	1 tsp.	5 mL
Paprika	$1/16$ tsp.	0.5 mL
Reserved mushroom caps		

Twist stems from mushrooms. Reserve caps. Chop stems.

Scramble-fry sausage meat and mushroom stems in frying pan until no pink remains in meat. Drain.

Mash cream cheese with bread crumbs and paprika. Add sausage mixture. Mix well. Stuff mushroom caps. Arrange in small shallow pan. Broil for 5 to 6 minutes. Makes 6.

1 stuffed mushroom contains: 36 Calories (152 kJ); 3 g Fat; 1 g Protein; 46 mg Sodium

DIPPER DILL

Easy to make at the last minute so you can relax and enjoy after a busy day.

Salad dressing (or mayonnaise)	$1/3$ cup	75 mL
Sour cream	$1/4$ cup	60 mL
Parsley flakes	1 tsp.	5 mL
Dill weed	$1/2$ tsp.	2 mL
Onion powder	$1/8$ tsp.	0.5 mL
Celery salt	$1/16$ tsp.	0.5 mL
Salt	$1/16$ tsp.	0.5 mL
Vegetable pieces		
Assorted chips		

Mix first 7 ingredients in small bowl. Chill until ready to use.

Serve with dippers such as assorted vegetables and/or chips. Makes $1/2$ cup (125 mL).

1 tbsp. (15 mL) contains: 61 Calories (254 kJ); 5.9 g Fat; trace Protein; 95 mg Sodium

SAUSAGE HORS D'OEUVRES

Little sausage biscuit balls make for a tasty appetizer.

Sausage meat	¼ lb.	113 g
Grated medium or sharp Cheddar cheese	½ cup	125 mL
Biscuit mix	⅔ cup	150 mL

Mix sausage meat with cheese in bowl. Add biscuit mix gradually, mixing well. You will need to work this with your hands. If too dry, add about ½ tsp. (2 mL) water at a time and work in. Shape into 1 tbsp. (15 mL) balls. Arrange on greased baking sheet. Bake in 375°F (190°C) oven for about 20 minutes until browned. Makes 15.

1 hors d'oeuvre contains: 55 Calories (232 kJ); 3.4 g Fat; 2 g Protein; 131 mg Sodium

Pictured on page 125.

SWISS MOCHA

A milky coffee drink to end a meal or to sip by the fireplace.

Skim milk powder	⅓ cup	75 mL
Granulated sugar	1 tbsp.	15 mL
Instant coffee granules	2 tsp.	10 mL
Cocoa	2 tsp.	10 mL
Boiling water	2 cups	500 mL
Whipped cream or frozen whipped topping, thawed (optional), for garnish		

Measure first 4 ingredients into small bowl. Stir. Divide between 2 mugs, each holding 9 oz. (250 mL).

Fill mugs with boiling water. Stir. Makes 2 cups (500 mL).

Top with whipped cream or other topping to make this special.

1 cup (250 mL) contains: 108 Calories (453 kJ); trace Fat; 8 g Protein; 114 mg Sodium

Pictured on page 71.

MIMOSA

Increase this recipe for one as many times as required. Orange flavored with a twist.

Prepared orange juice	**½ cup**	**125 mL**
Champagne (or white grape juice)	**¼ cup**	**60 mL**

Pour chilled orange juice and champagne into stemmed glass. Stir gently. Makes 1 mimosa.

1 mimosa contains: 100 Calories (420 kJ); trace Fat; 1 g Protein; 4 mg Sodium

Pictured on front cover.

MULLED CIDER

An aromatic drink for two. Serve with cinnamon "stir" sticks.

Apple juice	**2¼ cups**	**560 mL**
Whole cloves	**3**	**3**
Cinnamon stick, about 2 inches (5 cm) long	**1**	**1**

Combine all 3 ingredients in saucepan. Heat until just boiling. Simmer for 5 minutes. Divide between 2 mugs. Makes 1½ cups (375 mL). Serves 2.

1 serving contains: 140 Calories (587 kJ); trace Fat; trace Protein; 9 mg Sodium

Pictured on page 17.

ORANGE JULIUS

Frothy and cool. Great on a hot day or even on a cold day.

Prepared orange juice	**1½ cups**	**375 mL**
Skim milk powder	**¼ cup**	**60 mL**
Granulated sugar	**2 tsp.**	**10 mL**
Vanilla	**½ tsp.**	**2 mL**
Crushed ice (about 4 cubes)	**½ cup**	**125 mL**

Put all 5 ingredients into blender. Process until smooth. Divide between 2 tall glasses. Makes 2½ cups (625 mL), enough for 2 servings.

1 serving contains: 163 Calories (684 kJ); trace Fat; 7 g Protein; 87 mg Sodium

COOL CHOCOLATE MINT

Chocolate and mint make for an excellent flavor.

Skim milk (or 2%)	2 cups	500 mL
Chocolate syrup	2 tbsp.	30 mL
Skim milk powder	$1/2$ cup	125 mL
Peppermint flavoring	$1/4$ tsp.	1 mL

Beat all 4 ingredients together in extra large measuring cup or medium bowl. Pour into two 9 oz. (250 mL) mugs. Makes 2 cups (500 mL).

1 cup (250 mL) contains: 252 Calories (1054 kJ); 1.1 g Fat; 21 g Protein; 313 mg Sodium

BRAN MUFFINS

Raisins lend their flavor to these popular muffins.

Large egg	1	1
Cooking oil	$1^1/2$ tbsp.	25 mL
Brown sugar (or granulated)	3 tbsp.	50 mL
Raisins	$1/3$ cup	75 mL
Milk	$1/4$ cup	60 mL
White vinegar	1 tsp.	5 mL
All bran cereal (100%)	$1/2$ cup	125 mL
All-purpose flour	$2/3$ cup	150 mL
Baking soda	$1/4$ tsp.	1 mL
Baking powder	$1/4$ tsp.	1 mL
Salt	$1/16$ tsp.	0.5 mL

Mix egg, cooking oil, brown sugar and raisins in bowl.

Stir milk and vinegar in cup. Let stand for 3 minutes. Add. Stir.

Measure remaining 5 ingredients into separate bowl. Stir. Add. Stir just to mix. Divide among 6 greased muffin cups. Bake in 400°F (205°C) oven for about 15 minutes. An inserted wooden pick should come out clean. Let stand for 5 minutes before removing from pan. Makes 6 medium muffins.

1 muffin contains: 175 Calories (734 kJ); 5.2 g Fat; 4 g Protein; 157 mg Sodium

Pictured on page 35.

DATE LOAF

This is probably one of the first loaves to grace tea tables.

Chopped dates	1/2 cup	125 mL
Granulated sugar	1/2 cup	125 mL
Butter or hard margarine	2 tbsp.	30 mL
Boiling water	1/2 cup	125 mL
All-purpose flour	1 1/4 cups	300 mL
Baking powder	1/2 tsp.	2 mL
Baking soda	1/2 tsp.	2 mL
Salt	1/2 tsp.	2 mL
Large egg, fork-beaten	1	1
Vanilla	1/2 tsp.	2 mL
Chopped walnuts or pecans (optional)	1/3 cup	75 mL

Combine first 4 ingredients in large bowl. Stir. Let stand until cool.

Add flour, baking powder, baking soda and salt. Stir.

Stir in egg, vanilla and walnuts. Turn into greased 7³/₄ x 3³/₄ x 2¹/₈ inch (19.5 x 9.5 x 5.5 cm) foil loaf pan. Bake in 350°F (175°C) oven for about 50 minutes until an inserted wooden pick comes out clean. Cuts into 8 slices.

1 slice contains: 188 Calories (789 kJ); 4 g Fat; 3.8 g Protein; 295 mg Sodium

SCONES

Sprinkled with sugar. These are a bit crusted with a nice texture.

All-purpose flour	2/3 cup	150 mL
Granulated sugar	1 tbsp.	15 mL
Baking powder	1 1/2 tsp.	7 mL
Salt	1/8 tsp.	0.5 mL
Cold butter or hard margarine	1 1/2 tbsp.	25 mL
Large egg	1	1
Skim evaporated milk (or light cream)	1 tbsp.	15 mL
Milk, for brushing top		
Granulated sugar, for top		

(continued on next page)

Measure first 4 ingredients into bowl. Cut in butter until crumbly.

Beat egg and milk together in small bowl. Add to flour mixture. Stir to form a ball. Pat into a round flat scone 1 inch (2.5 cm) thick. Place on greased baking sheet. Score top into 4 sections.

Brush with milk. Sprinkle with sugar. Bake in 400°F (205°C) oven for 12 to 15 minutes. Cuts into 4 wedges.

1 wedge contains: 159 Calories (444 kJ); 6.3 g Fat; 4 g Protein; 165 mg Sodium

Pictured on page 35.

RHUBARB MUFFINS

Well-rounded muffins. Mild flavor.

Cooking oil	1¹⁄₂ tbsp.	25 mL
Large egg	1	1
Brown sugar, packed	¹⁄₃ cup	75 mL
Granulated sugar	1 tbsp.	15 mL
Vanilla	¹⁄₂ tsp.	2 mL
Milk	¹⁄₄ cup	60 mL
White vinegar	1 tsp.	5 mL
Cubed rhubarb, fresh or frozen (thawed), ¹⁄₄ inch (6 mm) size	¹⁄₂ cup	125 mL
Chopped walnuts, optional	2 tbsp.	30 mL
All-purpose flour	1 cup	250 mL
Baking powder	¹⁄₄ tsp.	1 mL
Baking soda	¹⁄₄ tsp.	1 mL
Salt	¹⁄₁₆ tsp.	0.5 mL

Beat first 5 ingredients together in bowl.

Mix milk and vinegar in cup. Let stand 3 to 4 minutes. Add to first mixture. Stir.

Add rhubarb and walnuts. Stir.

Stir remaining 4 ingredients together. Add. Stir just to moisten. Divide among 6 greased muffin cups. Bake in 400°F (205°C) oven for about 15 minutes. An inserted wooden pick should come out clean. Let stand 5 minutes before removing from pan. Makes 6 medium muffins.

1 muffin contains: 192 Calories (801 kJ); 5.1 g Fat; 4 g Protein; 106 mg Sodium

Pictured on page 35.

BUTTERMILK PANCAKES

Makes good "from scratch" pancakes.

Large egg	1	1
Buttermilk, fresh or reconstituted from powder	1¼ cups	300 mL
Cooking oil	1½ tbsp.	25 mL
All-purpose flour	1¼ cups	300 mL
Granulated sugar	1 tbsp.	15 mL
Baking powder	1½ tsp.	7 mL
Baking soda	½ tsp.	2 mL
Salt	½ tsp.	2 mL

Beat egg with spoon in bowl. Add buttermilk and cooking oil. Stir.

Measure remaining 5 ingredients into separate bowl. Stir. Make a well in center. Pour egg mixture into well. Stir just to moisten. Heat electric griddle or frying pan to 380°F (190°C). Test by adding a few drops of cold water to pan. They should dance all over the pan rather just sizzle. Fry ¼ cup (60 mL) on greased pan. When bubbles form and edges appear dry, turn to brown other side. Makes 9 pancakes.

1 pancake contains: 119 Calories (497 kJ); 3.6 g Fat; 4 g Protein; 275 mg Sodium

1. White Batter Bread, page 28
2. Mulled Cider, page 12
3. Shrimp Mousse, page 8
4. Tangy Caesar Salad, page 128
5. Coq Au Vin, page 96

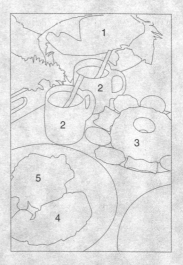

Tray Courtesy Of:
La Cache

Napkins & Napkin Rings Courtesy Of:
La Cache

Basket Courtesy Of:
Wicker World

Mugs Courtesy Of:
The Bay Housewares Dept.

China Courtesy Of:
Eaton's China Dept.

CHEESE BISCUITS

Yummy biscuits, rich and tender. Best served warm.

All-purpose flour	1 cup	250 mL
Baking powder	1½ tsp.	7 mL
Baking soda	½ tsp.	2 mL
Granulated sugar	1 tsp.	5 mL
Salt	¼ tsp.	1 mL
Butter or hard margarine	¼ cup	60 mL
Sour cream	½ cup	125 mL
Grated medium or sharp Cheddar cheese, lightly packed	⅓ cup	75 mL

Measure first 5 ingredients into bowl. Cut in butter until crumbly.

Add sour cream and cheese. Stir into a ball. Knead 6 to 8 times. Roll or pat on lightly floured surface to ¾ inch (2 cm) thickness. Cut into 2 inch (5 cm) circles. Arrange on ungreased baking pan. Bake in 450°F (230°C) oven for about 12 minutes. Makes 7 biscuits.

1 biscuit contains: 184 Calories (768 kJ); 11.5g Fat; 4 g Protein; 313 mg Sodium

CORN MUFFINS

A yellow muffin. Best served warm.

All-purpose flour	½ cup	125 mL
Yellow cornmeal	½ cup	125 mL
Granulated sugar	2 tbsp.	30 mL
Baking powder	2 tsp.	10 mL
Salt	½ tsp.	2 mL
Butter or hard margarine	2 tbsp.	30 mL
Large egg	1	1
Milk	⅓ cup	75 mL

Measure first 5 ingredients into bowl. Cut in butter until crumbly.

Beat egg and milk together in separate bowl. Add. Stir just to moisten. Divide among 6 greased muffin cups. Bake in 400°F (205°C) oven for about 15 minutes. An inserted wooden pick should come out clean. Let stand for 5 minutes before removing from pan. Makes 6 medium muffins.

1 muffin contains: 157 Calories (656 kJ); 5.3 g Fat; 4 g Protein; 290 mg Sodium

Pictured on front cover.

COCONUT BISCUITS

Threads of coconut peek out of these. Different.

All-purpose flour	1 cup	250 mL
Granulated sugar	1½ tsp.	7 mL
Baking powder	1½ tsp.	7 mL
Salt	¼ tsp.	1 mL
Butter or hard margarine, softened	2 tbsp.	30 mL
Long thread coconut	⅓ cup	75 mL
Milk	6 tbsp.	100 mL

Mix first 5 ingredients together in bowl until crumbly.

Add coconut and milk. Stir into a ball. Knead 6 to 8 times. Roll or pat 3/4 inch (2 cm) thick on lightly floured surface. Cut into 2 inch (5 cm) circles. Arrange on greased baking sheet. Bake in 425°F (220°C) oven for about 12 minutes. Makes 6 biscuits.

1 biscuit contains: *162 Calories (679 kJ); 7.8 g Fat; 3 g Protein; 167 mg Sodium*

Pictured on page 125.

STREUSEL COFFEE CAKE

The streusel topping is the "icing on the cake".

STREUSEL

Butter or hard margarine	2 tsp.	10 mL
Brown sugar	2 tbsp.	30 mL
All-purpose flour	1½ tsp.	7 mL
Ground cinnamon	¼ tsp.	1 mL
Chopped walnuts or pecans (optional)	2 tbsp.	30 mL

CAKE

Butter or hard margarine, softened	2 tbsp.	30 mL
Granulated sugar	¼ cup	60 mL
Large egg	1	1
All-purpose flour	¾ cup	175 mL
Baking powder	½ tsp.	2 mL
Salt	⅛ tsp.	0.5 mL
Milk	⅓ cup	75 mL

(continued on next page)

Streusel: Melt butter in small saucepan. Stir in sugar, flour, cinnamon and walnuts.

Cake: Beat butter, sugar and egg together in bowl.

Stir flour, baking powder and salt together in small bowl. Add ¹/₂ to batter. Stir to moisten.

Stir in milk. Add second ¹/₂ flour mixture. Stir to moisten. Turn into greased 7³/₄ x 3³/₄ x 2¹/₈ inch (19.5 x 9.5 x 5.5 cm) foil loaf pan. Sprinkle streusel over top. Bake in 350°F (175°C) oven for 25 to 30 minutes. An inserted wooden pick should come out clean. Makes 8 slices.

1 slice contains: 135 Calories (565 kJ); 4.9 g Fat; 3 g Protein; 99 mg Sodium

Pictured on page 35.

TEA BISCUITS

Serve these tender biscuits warm or cold.

All-purpose flour	1 cup	250 mL
Granulated sugar	1 tbsp.	15 mL
Baking powder	1¹/₂ tsp.	7 mL
Salt	¹/₄ tsp.	1 mL
Butter or hard margarine	3 tbsp.	50 mL
Cooking oil	1 tbsp.	15 mL
Milk	¹/₄ cup	60 mL
Skim evaporated milk (or more milk)	2 tbsp.	30 mL

Mix flour, sugar, baking powder and salt together in bowl. Add butter and cooking oil. Cut in butter until mixture is crumbly.

Add both kinds of milk. Stir to form a ball. Knead 6 to 8 times. Roll or pat on lightly floured surface ³/₄ inch (2 cm) thick. Cut into 2 inch (5 cm) circles. Arrange on ungreased baking pan. Bake in 450°F (230°C) oven for about 12 minutes. Makes 6 biscuits.

1 biscuit contains: 171 Calories (717 kJ); 8.6 g Fat; 3 g Protein; 189 mg Sodium

APPLESAUCE LOAF

Darkish color and delicious.

Butter or hard margarine, softened	¼ cup	60 mL
Brown sugar, packed	⅓ cup	75 mL
Granulated sugar	1 tbsp.	15 mL
Large egg	1	1
Applesauce	⅔ cup	150 mL
All-purpose flour	1 cup	250 mL
Baking soda	½ tsp.	2 mL
Ground cinnamon	¼ tsp.	1 mL
Salt	¼ tsp.	1 mL
Chopped walnuts or raisins (optional)	¼ cup	60 mL

Cream butter and both sugars together in bowl. Beat in egg. Add applesauce. Mix.

Stir next 4 ingredients together in separate bowl. Add to batter. Stir.

Stir in walnuts or raisins. Turn into greased 7¾ x 3¾ x 2⅛ inch (19.5 x 9.5 x 5.5 cm) foil loaf pan. Bake in 350°F (175°C) oven for about 45 minutes until an inserted wooden pick comes out clean. Cuts into 8 slices.

1 slice contains: 175 Calories (732 kJ); 6.9 g Fat; 3 g Protein; 244 mg Sodium

BANANA LOAF

A nice moist loaf with a good banana flavor.

Butter or hard margarine, softened	¼ cup	60 mL
Granulated sugar	⅓ cup	75 mL
Large egg	1	1
Mashed banana	½ cup	125 mL
Sour milk (½ tsp., 2 mL white vinegar plus milk to make)	2 tbsp.	30 mL
All-purpose flour	1¼ cups	300 mL
Baking soda	½ tsp.	2 mL
Salt	¼ tsp.	1 mL
Chopped walnuts (optional)	¼ cup	60 mL

(continued on next page)

Cream butter and sugar in bowl. Beat in egg. Add banana and sour milk. Mix.

Stir flour, baking soda and salt together in small bowl. Add. Stir just to moisten.

Stir in walnuts. Turn into greased $7^3/_4$ x $3^3/_4$ x $2^1/_8$ inch (19.5 x 9.5 x 5.5 cm) foil loaf pan. Bake in 350°F (175°C) oven for about 40 minutes until an inserted wooden pick comes out clean. Cuts into 8 slices.

1 slice contains: 188 Calories (786 kJ); 7.1 g Fat; 3 g Protein; 243 mg Sodium

ZUCCHINI LOAF

Very flavorful and spicy.

Large egg	1	1
Cooking oil	$^1/_3$ cup	75 mL
Granulated sugar	$^2/_3$ cup	150 mL
Vanilla	$^1/_2$ tsp.	2 mL
Peeled, grated and drained zucchini	$^2/_3$ cup	150 mL
All-purpose flour	1 cup	250 mL
Ground cinnamon	1 tsp.	5 mL
Salt	$^1/_4$ tsp.	1 mL
Baking soda	$^1/_4$ tsp.	1 mL
Baking powder	$^1/_4$ tsp.	1 mL
Chopped walnuts or pecans (optional)	$^1/_3$ cup	75 mL

Beat egg, cooking oil, sugar and vanilla in bowl.

Stir in zucchini.

Stir remaining ingredients together in small bowl. Add to batter. Stir just until moistened. Turn into greased $7^3/_4$ x $3^3/_4$ x $2^1/_8$ inch (19.5 x 9.5 x 5.5 cm) foil loaf pan. Bake in 350°F (175°C) oven for about 1 hour until an inserted wooden pick comes out clean. Makes 1 small loaf. Cuts into 8 slices.

1 slice contains: 225 Calories (943 kJ); 10.4 g Fat; 3 g Protein; 137 mg Sodium

SAUSAGE STUFFING BALLS

Such a handy way to serve stuffing.

Butter or hard margarine	1 tsp.	5 mL
Lean pork sausage meat	½ lb.	227 g
Chopped onion	⅔ cup	150 mL
Chopped celery	½ cup	125 mL
Large egg	1	1
Poultry seasoning	¾ tsp.	4 mL
Parsley flakes	1 tsp.	5 mL
Chicken bouillon powder	1½ tsp.	7 mL
Cayenne pepper	⅛ tsp.	0.5 mL
Salt, sprinkle		
Pepper, sprinkle		
Water	1 cup	250 mL
Croutons	1½ cups	375 mL
Butter or hard margarine	5 tsp.	25 mL

Melt first amount of butter in frying pan. Add sausage meat, onion and celery. Sauté until no pink remains in meat. Drain.

Beat egg in bowl. Add next 6 ingredients. Beat. Add to onion mixture. Stir.

Add water. Stir until mixture boils. Remove from heat.

Stir in croutons. Let stand 5 minutes. Shape into balls using ½ cup (125 mL) each. Arrange in greased pan.

Top each ball with 1 tsp. (5 mL) butter. Bake in 325°F (160°C) oven for 30 minutes. Makes 5 stuffing balls.

1 stuffing ball contains: *198 Calories (826 kJ); 13.1 g Fat; 8 g Protein; 657 mg Sodium*

Paré Pointer

A fuzzy caterpillar is an upholstered worm.

No kneading required. Just the pleasant task of consuming.

Granulated sugar	1 tsp.	5 mL
Warm water	1¼ cups	300 mL
Envelope active dry yeast (or 1 tbsp.,15 mL)	1 x ¼ oz.	1 x 8 g
Whole wheat flour	2 cups	500 mL
Cooking oil	2 tbsp.	30 mL
Mild molasses	2 tbsp.	30 mL
Salt	1 tsp.	5 mL
All-purpose flour	1 cup	250 mL

Stir sugar into warm water in large bowl. Sprinkle yeast over top. Let stand for 10 minutes. Stir to dissolve yeast.

Add next 4 ingredients. Beat on low to moisten. Beat on medium-high for 2 minutes.

Work in remaining flour. Cover with greased waxed paper and tea towel. Let stand in oven with light on and door closed for 40 to 45 minutes until doubled in bulk. Stir batter down. Spoon into greased 8 x 4 x 3 inch (20 x 10 x 7 cm) glass loaf pan. Cover with greased waxed paper and tea towel. Let stand in oven with light on and door closed for about 20 minutes until doubled in size or just up to top edge of pan. Bake in 375°F (190°C) oven for 25 to 30 minutes. Makes 1 loaf. Cuts into 16 slices.

1 slice contains: 108 Calories (452 kJ); 2.1 g Fat; 3 g Protein; 171 mg Sodium

Pictured on page 35.

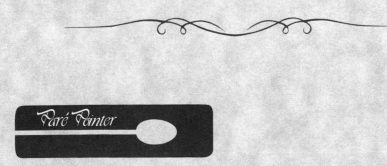

Paré Pointer

A sandwich man is just a quick snack for a cannibal.

SOUR CREAM COFFEE CAKE

A good rich cake with a nutty, sugary topping.

Butter or hard margarine, softened	¼ cup	60 mL
Granulated sugar	½ cup	125 mL
Large egg	1	1
Vanilla	½ tsp.	2 mL
Low-fat sour cream (7% MF)	½ cup	125 mL
All-purpose flour	1 cup	250 mL
Baking powder	½ tsp.	2 mL
Baking soda	½ tsp.	2 mL
Salt	⅛ tsp.	0.5 mL
FILLING AND TOPPING		
Brown sugar, packed	¼ cup	60 mL
Ground cinnamon	½ tsp.	2 mL
Finely chopped walnuts or pecans	2 tbsp.	30 mL

Cream butter and sugar in bowl. Add egg. Beat. Add vanilla and sour cream. Mix.

Stir in next 4 ingredients. Spread ½ batter in greased 8 x 4 x 3 inch (20 x 10 x 7 cm) glass loaf pan.

Filling And Topping: Mix sugar, cinnamon and walnuts in small bowl. Sprinkle ½ over batter in pan. Cover with second ½ batter by putting dabs here and there over topping. Spread as best you can. Cover with second ½ topping. Bake in 350°F (175°C) oven for about 30 minutes until an inserted wooden pick comes out clean. Cuts into 6 pieces.

1 piece contains: 306 Calories (1279 kJ); 12.3 g Fat; 4 g Protein; 281 mg Sodium

Pictured on page 35.

Paré Pointer

A nosebleed isn't such a big deal. Unless you're an elephant that is.

Good flavor with a pinkish tinge. When sliced, the cherries are so attractive.

Butter or hard margarine, softened	3 tbsp.	50 mL
Granulated sugar	$\frac{1}{2}$ cup	125 mL
Large egg	1	1
Almond flavoring	$\frac{1}{2}$ tsp.	2 mL
Vanilla	$\frac{1}{2}$ tsp.	2 mL
Chopped maraschino cherries, juice reserved	3 tbsp.	50 mL
Reserved cherry juice	2 tbsp.	30 mL
Prepared orange juice	2 tbsp.	30 mL
All-purpose flour	1 cup	250 mL
Baking powder	$\frac{1}{2}$ tsp.	2 mL
Salt	$\frac{1}{4}$ tsp.	1 mL

Cream butter and sugar in bowl. Beat in egg, almond flavoring and vanilla. Add cherries, cherry juice, and orange juice. Beat to mix.

Measure flour into small bowl. Stir in baking powder and salt. Add to batter. Stir just to moisten. Turn into greased $7\frac{3}{4}$ x $3\frac{3}{4}$ x $2\frac{1}{8}$ inch (19.5 x 9.5 x 5.5 cm) foil loaf pan. Bake in 350°F (175°C) oven for about 45 minutes until an inserted wooden pick comes out clean. Cuts into 8 slices.

1 slice contains: *174 Calories (730 kJ); 5.2 g Fat; 3 g Protein; 139 mg Sodium*

CHERRY NUT LOAF: Add $\frac{1}{4}$ cup (60 mL) chopped walnuts or pecans.

A hungry beast longs to eat. A greedy beast eats too long.

WHITE BATTER BREAD

Enjoy the aroma and taste of fresh bread without the work of kneading.

Granulated sugar	1 tsp.	5 mL
Warm water	1¼ cups	300 mL
Envelope active dry yeast (or 1 tbsp., 15 mL)	1 x ¼ oz.	1 x 8 g
All-purpose flour	2 cups	500 mL
Cooking oil	2 tbsp.	30 mL
Granulated sugar	1 tbsp.	15 mL
Salt	1 tsp.	5 mL
All-purpose flour	1 cup	250 mL

Stir first amount of sugar into warm water in large warmed bowl to dissolve sugar. Sprinkle yeast over top. Let stand 10 minutes. Stir.

Add next 4 ingredients. Beat on low to moisten. Beat on medium-high for 2 minutes.

Work in remaining flour. Cover with tea towel. Let stand in oven with light on and door closed for about 40 minutes until doubled in bulk. Stir batter down. Spoon into greased 8 x 4 x 3 inch (20 x 10 x 7 cm) glass loaf pan. Cover with greased waxed paper and tea towel. Let stand in oven with light on and door closed for about 20 minutes until doubled in size or just up to edge of pan. Bake in 375°F (190°C) oven for 25 to 30 minutes. Makes 1 loaf. Cuts into 16 slices.

1 slice contains: 111 Calories (464 kJ); 2 g Fat; 3 g Protein; 170 mg Sodium

Pictured on page 17.

CREAM CHEESE ICING

A partner for Carrot Cake, page 40. Also good on Chocolate Cake, page 32.

Cream cheese, softened (¼ cup, 60 mL)	½ x 4 oz.	½ x 125 g
Icing (confectioner's) sugar	1 cup	250 mL
Vanilla	½ tsp.	2 mL

Beat all 3 ingredients together well in small bowl until smooth. Makes ½ cup (125 mL).

1 tbsp. (15 mL) contains: 84 Calories (349 kJ); 2.6 g Fat; 1 g Protein; 22 mg Sodium

Pictured on page 53.

SPICED APPLESAUCE CAKE

Darkish color and a good match for Caramel Icing, below.

Butter or hard margarine, softened	¼ cup	60 mL
Granulated sugar	½ cup	125 mL
Brown sugar, packed	½ cup	125 mL
Large egg	1	1
Applesauce	⅔ cup	150 mL
Vanilla	¼ tsp.	1 mL
All-purpose flour	1¼ cups	300 mL
Baking soda	¾ tsp.	4 mL
Ground cinnamon	¼ tsp.	1 mL
Ground nutmeg	⅛ tsp.	0.5 mL
Ground cloves	⅛ tsp.	0.5 mL
Salt (optional)	¼ tsp.	1 mL

Caramel Icing, below

Beat first 4 ingredients together in bowl.

Mix in applesauce and vanilla.

Measure remaining 6 ingredients into separate bowl. Stir. Add. Stir to moisten. Turn into greased 7 × 7 inch (18 × 18 cm) foil pan. Bake in 350°F (175°C) oven for 35 to 45 minutes until an inserted wooden pick comes out clean. Cool. Ice with Caramel Icing. Cuts into 9 pieces.

1 piece contains: 225 Calories (943 kJ); 6.2 g Fat; 3 g Protein; 182 mg Sodium

CARAMEL ICING

Excellent on Spiced Applesauce Cake, above, as well as white cakes.

Icing (confectioner's) sugar	1 cup	250 mL
Butter or hard margarine, softened	1½ tbsp.	25 mL
Vanilla	¼ tsp.	1 mL
Caramel sundae topping	¼ cup	60 mL

Beat all ingredients together. You may need to add a bit more icing sugar or sundae topping to get proper spreading consistency. Makes ⅔ cup (150 mL).

1 tbsp. (15 mL) contains: 81 Calories (341 kJ); 1.9 g Fat; trace Protein; 20 mg Sodium

CHERRY CAKE

A showy cake with cherries peeking through.

Butter or hard margarine, softened	1/3 cup	75 mL
Granulated sugar	1/2 cup	125 mL
Large eggs	2	2
Almond flavoring	1/4 tsp.	1 mL
All-purpose flour	1 cup	250 mL
Baking powder	1/2 tsp.	2 mL
Finely ground almonds	1/4 cup	60 mL
Glazed cherries, halved	1/3 cup	75 mL

Almond Icing, below

Cream butter and sugar together in bowl. Beat in eggs, 1 at a time. Add almond flavoring.

Stir in next 4 ingredients. Turn into greased 7 x 7 inch (18 x 18 cm) foil pan. Bake in 350°F (175°C) oven for 35 to 40 minutes until an inserted wooden pick comes out clean. Cool.

Ice with Almond Icing. Makes 1 small cake. Cuts into 9 pieces.

1 piece contains: 219 Calories (916 kJ); 9.9 g Fat; 4 g Protein; 89 mg Sodium

BUTTER ICING

Use to ice white or spice cakes. Especially good on Coconut Cake, page 37.

Icing (confectioner's) sugar	1 cup	250 mL
Butter or hard margarine, softened	1 1/2 tbsp.	25 mL
Milk	1 1/2 tbsp.	25 mL
Vanilla	1/4 tsp.	1 mL

Beat all ingredients together in bowl. Add more icing sugar or milk to make good spreading consistency. Makes 1/2 cup (125 mL).

1 tbsp. (15 mL) contains: 74 Calories (309 kJ); 2.4 g Fat; trace Protein; 25 mg Sodium

ALMOND ICING: Omit vanilla. Stir in 1/4 tsp. (1 mL) almond flavoring. Use to ice Cherry Cake, above.

A neat little cake, and so good.

White cake mix, 1 layer size	½	½
Instant vanilla pudding powder,	½	½
4 serving size		
Large egg	1	1
Cooking oil	2 tbsp.	30 mL
Water	2 tbsp.	30 mL
Sour cream	¼ cup	60 mL
Semisweet chocolate chips	½ cup	125 mL
GLAZE		
Icing (confectioner's) sugar	1 cup	250 mL
Water	4 tsp.	20 mL
Cocoa	1 tsp.	5 mL
Vanilla	⅛ tsp.	0.5 mL
Water	⅛ tsp.	0.5 mL

Place first 5 ingredients in bowl. Beat on medium until smooth.

Stir in sour cream and chocolate chips. Turn into greased and floured 4 cup (1 L) tube pan (or mold). Bake in 350°F (175°C) oven for about 40 minutes until an inserted wooden pick comes out clean. Let stand 10 to 15 minutes. Turn out of pan. Cool and glaze.

Glaze: Stir icing sugar and first amount of water together, adding a bit more of either if needed to make a barely pourable consistency. Spoon ⅔ of glaze over cake allowing some to run down sides.

Stir cocoa and vanilla into remaining glaze. Add a touch of water as needed for proper consistency. Drizzle over white glaze. Makes 1 cake. Cuts into 6 pieces.

1 piece contains: *322 Calories (1347 kJ); 13.5 g Fat; 3 g Protein; 116 mg Sodium*

Pictured on front cover.

Paré Pointer

A minor wound is really a short cut.

BOILED ICING

Try a cooked icing. Yellow, smooth and rich.

Butter or hard margarine	½ cup	125 mL
Granulated sugar	¼ cup	60 mL
Large egg	1	1
Icing (confectioner's) sugar	¾ cup	175 mL

Put butter and sugar into small saucepan. Heat and stir until butter melts.

Add egg. Mix well. Stir for about 5 minutes until mixture comes to a boil. Remove from heat. Cool.

Add icing sugar. Stir. Makes 1 cup (250 mL), enough to ice top and sides of small cake.

1 tbsp. (15 mL) contains: 88 Calories (367 kJ); 6.1 g Fat; trace Protein; 63 mg Sodium

CHOCOLATE CAKE

A one bowl cake. So easy.

Butter or hard margarine, softened	¼ cup	60 mL
Granulated sugar	½ cup	125 mL
All-purpose flour	⅞ cup	200 mL
Cocoa	2 tbsp.	30 mL
Baking soda	½ tsp.	2 mL
Salt	¼ tsp.	1 mL
Large egg	1	1
Water	½ cup	125 mL
Vanilla	½ tsp.	2 mL

Measure all ingredients into bowl. Beat until smooth. Turn into greased 7 x 7 inch (18 x 18 cm) foil pan. Bake in 350°F (175°C) oven for 30 to 35 minutes. An inserted wooden pick comes out clean. Cool. Ice with Chocolate Icing, page 37. Cuts into 9 pieces.

1 piece contains: 151 Calories (632 kJ); 6.2 g Fat; 2 g Protein; 214 mg Sodium

DATE NUT CHIP CAKE

A bit larger cake but even so, it will go fast. No icing needed as it has a nut and chocolate chip topping.

Chopped dates	½ cup	125 mL
Baking soda	½ tsp.	2 mL
Boiling water	⅔ cup	150 mL
Butter or hard margarine, softened	6 tbsp.	100 mL
Granulated sugar	½ cup	125 mL
Large egg	1	1
Vanilla	½ tsp.	2 mL
All-purpose flour	⅞ cup	200 mL
Baking powder	½ tsp.	2 mL
Salt, large measure	¼ tsp.	1 mL
TOPPING		
Semisweet chocolate chips	½ cup	125 mL
Chopped walnuts	¼ cup	60 mL

Combine dates, baking soda and boiling water in bowl. Let stand to cool.

Cream butter and sugar together in bowl. Beat in egg and vanilla. Stir in date mixture.

Mix flour, baking powder and salt in separate bowl. Add. Stir to moisten. Turn into greased 8 x 8 inch (20 x 20 cm) pan.

Topping: Sprinkle with chocolate chips and walnuts. Bake in 350°F (175°C) oven for about 40 minutes. An inserted wooden pick should come out clean. Cool. Cuts into 16 pieces.

1 piece contains: 145 Calories (608 kJ);7.7 g Fat; 2 g Protein; 135 mg Sodium

Paré Pointer

"Although I wasn't speeding, Officer, I passed two drivers who were!"

WHITE CAKE

Golden colored cake with a choice of icings.

Butter or hard margarine	$1/4$ cup	60 mL
Granulated sugar	$1/2$ cup	125 mL
White corn syrup	1 tbsp.	15 mL
Vanilla	$1/2$ tsp.	2 mL
Large egg	1	1
Milk	$1/2$ cup	125 mL
All-purpose flour	1 cup	250 mL
Baking powder	1 tsp.	5 mL
Salt	$1/4$ tsp.	1 mL

Combine first 4 ingredients in saucepan. Heat and stir until butter melts. Cool.

Beat in egg. Add milk. Stir.

Measure flour, baking powder and salt into small bowl. Stir. Add. Stir until smooth. Turn into greased 7 x 7 inch (18 x 18 cm) foil pan. Bake in 350°F (175°C) oven for about 35 minutes until an inserted wooden pick comes out clean. Cool. Ice with Butter Icing, page 30, Caramel Icing, page 29 or Chocolate Icing, page 37. Cuts into 9 pieces.

1 piece contains: 170 Calories (711 kJ); 6.4 g Fat; 3 g Protein; 149 mg Sodium

1. Sour Cream Coffee Cake, page 26
2. Brown Batter Bread, page 25
3. Scones, page 14
4. Streusel Coffee Cake, page 20
5. Rhubarb Muffins, page 15
6. Bran Muffins, page 13

Background Tile Courtesy Of:
Tile Town

Basket Courtesy Of:
Wicker World

Pottery Dishes Courtesy Of:
Clayworks Studios

Serving Platter/Tea Cups/Linens Courtesy Of:
La Cache

COCONUT CAKE

White in color with a mild coconut flavor.

Butter or hard margarine, softened	$^1/_4$ **cup**	**60 mL**
Granulated sugar	$^1/_2$ **cup**	**125 mL**
Large egg	**1**	**1**
All-purpose flour	**1 cup**	**250 mL**
Baking powder	**1 tsp.**	**5 mL**
Salt	$^1/_8$ **tsp.**	**0.5 mL**
Fine coconut	$^1/_4$ **cup**	**60 mL**
Milk	$^1/_4$ **cup**	**60 mL**

Cream butter, sugar and egg together well in bowl.

Combine next 4 ingredients in separate bowl. Stir. Add $^1/_2$ to creamed mixture. Stir.

Stir in milk. Add second $^1/_2$ flour mixture. Stir. Turn into greased 7 x 7 inch (18 x 18 cm) foil pan. Bake in 350°F (175°C) oven for 25 to 30 minutes until an inserted wooden pick comes out clean. Cool. Ice with Butter Icing, page 30. Cuts into 9 pieces.

1 piece contains: 177 Calories (739 kJ); 8 g Fat; 3 g Protein; 109 mg Sodium

CHOCOLATE ICING

Good chocolate flavor. Use on Chocolate Cake, page 32, or White Cake, page 34.

Icing (confectioner's) sugar	$^3/_4$ **cup**	**175 mL**
Cocoa	**2 tbsp.**	**30 mL**
Butter or hard margarine, softened	$1^1/_2$ **tbsp.**	**25 mL**
Milk	$1^1/_2$ **tbsp.**	**25 mL**
Vanilla	$^1/_4$ **tsp.**	**1 mL**

Beat all ingredients together in bowl. Add a bit more icing sugar or milk if needed to make proper spreading consistency. Makes $^1/_2$ cup (125 mL).

1 tbsp. (15 mL) contains: 64 Calories (267 kJ); 2.5 g Fat; trace Protein; 26 mg Sodium

POUND CAKE

Fine textured. Serve as is or with fruit and ice cream or with a sauce over it.

Butter or hard margarine, softened	¼ cup	60 mL
Granulated sugar	½ cup	125 mL
Large egg	1	1
Vanilla	¾ tsp.	4 mL
Lemon flavoring	¾ tsp.	4 mL
All-purpose flour	¾ cup	175 mL
Baking powder	⅛ tsp.	0.5 mL
Baking soda	⅛ tsp.	0.5 mL
Salt	¼ tsp.	1 mL
Milk	¼ cup	60 mL
White vinegar	1 tsp.	5 mL

Cream butter and sugar together in bowl. Beat in egg, vanilla and lemon flavoring.

Stir flour, baking powder, baking soda and salt together in separate bowl. Add ½ to butter mixture and stir.

Combine milk and vinegar in cup. Let stand 3 minutes. Mix into batter. Stir in second ½ of flour mixture. Turn into greased 7¾ x 3¾ x 2⅛ inch (19.5 x 9.5 x 5.5 cm) foil loaf pan. Bake in 350°F (175°C) oven for about 35 to 40 minutes. An inserted wooden pick should come out clean. Cuts into 10 slices.

1 slice contains: 133 Calories (557 kJ); 5.6 g Fat; 2 g Protein; 146 mg Sodium

Do knee caps help to keep your legs warm?

Comes from the oven with a ready made topping.

All-purpose flour	1 cup	250 mL
Ground cinnamon	½ tsp.	2 mL
Ground nutmeg	¼ tsp.	1 mL
Salt	¼ tsp.	1 mL
Brown sugar, packed	½ cup	125 mL
Granulated sugar	¼ cup	60 mL
Butter or hard margarine	6 tbsp.	100 mL
All-purpose flour	¼ cup	60 mL
Large egg	1	1
Buttermilk, fresh or reconstituted from powder	½ cup	125 mL
Vanilla	½ tsp.	2 mL
Raisins	½ cup	125 mL
Baking soda	½ tsp.	2 mL

Stir first 6 ingredients in medium bowl. Add butter. Cut in until crumbly. Reserve ½ cup (125 mL) for topping.

Add second amount of flour to first mixture. Stir.

Beat egg in separate bowl. Add buttermilk, vanilla, raisins and baking soda. Mix. Add to first mixture. Mix quickly. Turn into greased 7 x 7 inch (18 x 18 cm) foil pan. Sprinkle with reserved crumbs. Bake in 350°F (175°C) oven for 35 to 40 minutes until an inserted wooden pick comes out clean. Cool. Cuts into 9 pieces.

1 piece contains: 247 Calories (1035 kJ); 8.7 g Fat; 3 g Protein; 258 mg Sodium

Paré Pointer

A sand crab is really a grouchy person at the beach.

CARROT CAKE

Topping with Cream Cheese Icing makes this a short-lived cake.

Cooking oil	⅓ cup	75 mL
Granulated sugar	⅓ cup	75 mL
Large egg	1	1
Vanilla	¼ tsp.	1 mL
All-purpose flour	⅔ cup	150 mL
Baking soda	½ tsp.	2 mL
Baking powder	½ tsp.	2 mL
Ground cinnamon	½ tsp.	2 mL
Salt	¼ tsp.	1 mL
Grated carrot	¾ cup	175 mL

Cream Cheese Icing, page 28

Beat cooking oil, sugar, egg and vanilla together well in bowl.

Mix in flour, baking soda, baking powder, cinnamon and salt.

Stir in grated carrot. Turn into greased 7 x 7 inch (18 x 18 cm) foil pan. Bake in 350°F (175°C) oven for 35 to 40 minutes until an inserted wooded pick comes out clean. Cool.

Ice with Cream Cheese Icing. Cuts into 9 pieces.

1 piece contains: 154 Calories (645 kJ); 9.2 g Fat; 2 g Protein; 163 mg Sodium

Pictured on page 53.

SUGAR COOKIES

Flavored just right with almond. No rolling of dough required.

Butter or hard margarine, softened	½ cup	125 mL
Granulated sugar	¾ cup	175 mL
Large egg	1	1
Vanilla	1 tsp.	5 mL
Almond flavoring	½ tsp.	2 mL
All-purpose flour	2 cups	500 mL
Baking powder	1½ tsp.	7 mL
Salt	½ tsp.	2 mL

Granulated sugar, for topping

(continued on next page)

Cream butter and sugar together well. Beat in egg, vanilla and almond flavoring.

Add flour, baking powder and salt. Stir to mix well. Use 1 tbsp. (15 mL) to shape each ball. Arrange balls on greased cookie sheet.

Grease bottom of glass. Dip in sugar. Press ball flat. Repeat. Bake in 375°F (190°C) oven for 10 to 12 minutes. Makes about 25 cookies.

1 cookie contains: 101 Calories (424 kJ); 4.2 g Fat; 1 g Protein; 98 mg Sodium

OATMEAL CRISPIES

Nicely rounded with a crunchy good flavor.

Butter or hard margarine, softened	**¹/₂ cup**	**125 mL**
Granulated sugar	**¹/₂ cup**	**125 mL**
Brown sugar, packed	**¹/₂ cup**	**125 mL**
Large egg	**1**	**1**
White vinegar	**¹/₂ tsp.**	**2 mL**
Vanilla	**¹/₂ tsp.**	**2 mL**
Rolled oats (not instant)	**1¹/₄ cups**	**300 mL**
All-purpose flour	**1 cup**	**250 mL**
Baking soda	**¹/₂ tsp.**	**2 mL**

Measure first 6 ingredients into bowl. Beat well.

Mix in rolled oats, flour and baking soda. Drop by tablespoonfuls onto greased cookie sheet. Bake in 350°F (175°C) oven for 8 to 10 minutes. Makes about 32 cookies.

1 cookie contains: 83 Calories (349 kJ); 3.5 g Fat; 1 g Protein; 56 mg Sodium

Variation: About 2 to 3 tbsp. (30 to 50 mL) nuts, chocolate chips or raisins may be added.

Paré Pointer

Actually, jelly is only nervous jam.

CHOCOLATE MOSAIC COOKIES

Crunchy and crackly topped.

Butter or hard margarine, softened	2 tbsp.	30 mL
Granulated sugar	1/2 cup	125 mL
Large egg	1	1
Vanilla	1/2 tsp.	2 mL
All-purpose flour	1/2 cup	125 mL
Baking powder	1/2 tsp.	2 mL
Salt	1/16 tsp.	0.5 mL
Unsweetened chocolate baking square, cut up	1 × 1 oz.	1 × 28 g

Icing (confectioner's) sugar, for rolling

Beat butter, sugar, egg and vanilla together in small bowl.

Add flour, baking powder and salt. Mix in.

Melt chocolate in saucepan on low heat, stirring often. Stir into dough. Chill for at least 1 hour. Shape into 1 to 1 1/2 inch (2.5 to 3 cm) balls, using 1 tbsp. (15 mL) dough for each.

Roll balls in icing sugar. Arrange on greased cookie sheet. Bake in 350°F (175°C) oven for 10 to 12 minutes. Makes about 15 cookies.

1 cookie contains: 71 Calories (298 kJ); 2.7 g Fat; 1 g Protein; 32 mg Sodium

Pictured on page 53.

NUTTY COOKIES

Crunchy as well as nutty.

Butter or hard margarine, softened	1/4 cup	60 mL
Brown sugar, packed	3/4 cup	175 mL
Granulated sugar	1/4 cup	60 mL
Large egg	1	1
Vanilla	1/2 tsp.	2 mL
All-purpose flour	1 1/2 cups	375 mL
Baking soda	1/2 tsp.	2 mL
Salt	1/4 tsp.	1 mL
Chopped walnuts or pecans	1/2 cup	125 mL

Granulated sugar, for topping

(continued on next page)

Measure first 5 ingredients into bowl. Beat well.

Mix in flour, baking soda, salt and walnuts. Shape into 1 inch (2.5 cm) balls. Arrange balls on ungreased cookie sheet.

Press with greased bottom of glass dipped in granulated sugar. Bake in 375°F (175°C) oven for about 10 minutes. Makes 32 cookies.

1 cookie contains: 79 Calories (329 kJ); 3 g Fat; 1 g Protein; 62 mg Sodium

OATMEAL DROPS

Extra flavor with raisins and cinnamon.

Raisins	⅓ cup	75 mL
Boiling water, to cover		
Butter or hard margarine, softened	1½ tbsp.	25 mL
Granulated sugar	⅓ cup	75 mL
Large egg	1	1
Sour milk (1 tsp., 5 mL white vinegar plus milk)	¼ cup	60 mL
Vanilla	¼ tsp.	1 mL
All-purpose flour	¾ cup	175 mL
Rolled oats (not instant)	½ cup	125 mL
Ground cinnamon	½ tsp.	2 mL
Baking soda, scant measure	½ tsp.	2 mL
Salt	1/16 tsp.	0.5 mL
Chopped walnuts or pecans (optional)	3 tbsp.	50 mL

Combine raisins and boiling water in cup. Let stand 10 minutes to plump. Drain.

Beat butter, sugar and egg together in bowl. Add sour milk and vanilla. Mix. Add raisins. Stir.

Add remaining 6 ingredients. Mix. Drop by heaping teaspoonfuls onto greased cookie sheet. Bake in 375°F (190°C) oven for 10 to 12 minutes. Makes about 28 cookies.

1 cookie contains: 45 Calories (188 kJ); 1 g Fat; 1 g Protein; 41 mg Sodium

Pictured on page 53.

SOFT MOLASSES COOKIES

Soft to the bite. These are spicy and good with or without nuts.

Butter or hard margarine, softened	2 tbsp.	30 mL
Granulated sugar	2 tbsp.	30 mL
Large egg	1	1
Sour cream	2 tbsp.	30 mL
Mild molasses	2 tbsp.	30 mL
All-purpose flour	¾ cup	175 mL
Baking soda, large measure	⅛ tsp.	0.5 mL
Salt	¼ tsp.	1 mL
Ground cinnamon	⅛ tsp.	0.5 mL
Ground ginger	⅛ tsp.	0.5 mL
Ground nutmeg	⅛ tsp.	0.5 mL
Ground cloves	⅛ tsp.	0.5 mL
Chopped walnuts or pecans (optional)	2 tbsp.	30 mL

Mix butter, sugar and egg well. Add sour cream and molasses. Mix.

Add next 7 ingredients. Mix well.

Work walnuts into dough. Drop by heaping teaspoonfuls onto greased cookie sheet. Bake in 375°F (190°C) oven for about 10 minutes. Makes about 22 cookies.

1 cookie contains: *41 Calories (170 kJ); 1.5 g Fat; 1 g Protein; 54 mg Sodium*

Pictured on page 53.

CHOCOLATE CHIPPERS

Sweet and chocolaty.

Butter or hard margarine, softened	½ cup	125 mL
Brown sugar, packed	½ cup	125 mL
Large egg	1	1
Vanilla	½ tsp.	2 mL
All-purpose flour	1 cup	250 mL
More all-purpose flour	2 tbsp.	30 mL
Baking soda	½ tsp.	2 mL
Instant vanilla pudding powder, 4 serving size	½	½
Semisweet chocolate chips	1 cup	250 mL
Chopped walnuts (optional)	⅓ cup	75 mL

(continued on next page)

Cream butter and sugar together in bowl. Beat in egg and vanilla.

Add next 4 ingredients. Mix.

Add chocolate chips and walnuts. Work in. Shape into 1 inch (2.5 cm) balls. Arrange on ungreased cookie sheet. Flatten with flour coated bottom of glass. Flatten to 2 to 2¼ inch (5 to 6 cm) rounds. Bake in 350°F (175°C) oven for 15 to 18 minutes. Makes about 2 dozen.

1 cookie contains: 120 Calories (503 kJ); 6.5 g Fat; 1 g Protein; 82 mg Sodium

BREAD PUDDING

An old favorite topped with a brandy sauce.

Bread slices, buttered	4	4
Raisins, coarsely chopped	3 tbsp.	50 mL
Large egg	1	1
Granulated sugar	¼ cup	60 mL
Milk	1⅓ cups	325 mL
Vanilla	1 tsp.	5 mL
Salt	⅛ tsp.	0.5 mL
BRANDY SAUCE		
Granulated sugar	2 tbsp.	30 mL
All-purpose flour	1 tbsp.	15 mL
Milk	½ cup	125 mL
Vanilla	¼ tsp.	1 mL
Brandy flavoring	½ tsp.	2 mL

Cut bread into 1 inch (2.5 cm) squares. Put into greased 8 x 4 x 3 inch (20 x 10 x 7 cm) glass loaf pan. Sprinkle with raisins.

Beat egg in small bowl. Mix in sugar, milk, vanilla and salt. Pour over bread. Bake in 350°F (175°C) oven for about 40 minutes. A knife inserted halfway between edge and center should come out clean.

Brandy Sauce: Stir sugar and flour together in small saucepan. Stir in milk gradually so no lumps form. Add vanilla and brandy flavoring. Heat and stir until mixture boils and thickens. Makes ½ cup (125 mL). Spoon over pudding. Makes 4 servings (or 2 generous ones).

1 serving contains: 248 Calories (1038 kJ); 4.4 g Fat; 8 g Protein; 190 mg Sodium

BANANA CREAM DESSERT

The banana layer makes itself known in flavor. Creamy smooth dessert.

BOTTOM LAYER		
All-purpose flour	¾ cup	175 mL
Granulated sugar	1½ tsp.	7 mL
Butter or hard margarine, softened	3 tbsp.	50 mL
FILLING		
Medium banana, sliced	1	1
Instant vanilla pudding, 4 serving size	1	1
Milk	¾ cup	175 mL
Vanilla ice cream, softened	2 cups	500 mL
TOPPING		
Frozen whipped topping, thawed	¾ cup	175 mL
Reserved crumbs		

Bottom Layer: Mix flour, sugar and butter until crumbly. Reserve ¼ cup (60 mL). Press remaining crumbs in ungreased 7 x 7 inch (18 x 18 cm) foil pan. Place reserved crumbs loosely in separate pan. Bake bottom layer in 350°F (175°C) oven for 10 minutes. Bake crumbs for about 8 minutes until golden. Cool crust. Crumble reserved crumbs.

Filling: Arrange banana slices over bottom layer.

Beat pudding powder and milk together in small bowl until mixture thickens.

Add ice cream. Mix well. Pour over banana layer. Chill for 6 to 8 hours or overnight.

Topping: Spread topping over pudding mixture. Sprinkle with reserved toasted crumbs. Chill. Cuts into 6 pieces.

1 piece contains: 346 Calories (1446 kJ); 14.3 g Fat; 5 g Protein; 177 mg Sodium

Paré Pointer

And now for the dope on the weather, here's our favorite weatherman.

Blueberry cobbler is one of those good comfort desserts.

Blueberries, fresh or frozen	1 cup	250 mL
Granulated sugar	2 tbsp.	30 mL
Water	2 tbsp.	30 mL
Cornstarch	1 tsp.	5 mL
Water	1 tsp.	5 mL
TOPPING		
All-purpose flour	¼ cup	60 mL
Granulated sugar	1 tbsp.	15 mL
Baking powder	½ tsp.	2 mL
Salt	⅛ tsp.	0.5 mL
Cooking oil	4 tsp.	20 mL
Milk	2 tbsp.	30 mL
Vanilla	¼ tsp.	1 mL

Combine blueberries, sugar and first amount of water in small saucepan. Heat, stirring often, until mixture simmers. Simmer for 2 to 3 minutes until berries are cooked.

Mix cornstarch into second amount of water and stir into simmering berries. Stir until thickened a bit. Turn into ungreased 3 cup (750 mL) or 1 quart (1 L) casserole. Keep warm.

Topping: Measure first 4 ingredients into bowl. Stir.

Add cooking oil, milk and vanilla. Stir. Drop in 4 mounds over top. Bake, uncovered, in 400°F (205°C) oven for about 20 minutes. Serves 2.

1 serving contains: 274 Calories (1145 kJ); 10 g Fat; 3 g Protein; 194 mg Sodium

Paré Pointer

All kids would like to eat vegetables if they weren't supposed to.

CHOCOLATE WHIP

Rich, dark, smooth and great.

Butter or hard margarine	1 tsp.	5 mL
Semisweet chocolate chips	½ cup	125 mL
Granulated sugar	1 tsp.	5 mL
Vanilla	½ tsp.	2 mL
Salt, just a pinch		
Cornstarch	1½ tsp.	7 mL
Milk	6 tbsp.	100 mL
TOPPING		
Kahlua liqueur (optional)	2 tsp.	10 mL
Frozen whipped topping, thawed	⅓ cup	75 mL

Measure first 5 ingredients into blender. Set aside.

Stir cornstarch into milk in small saucepan. Heat and stir until boiling and thickened. Add to blender. Process until puréed. Pour into 2 custard cups. Chill.

Topping: Spoon 1 tsp. (5 mL) kahlua over each custard cup. Add whipped topping. Serves 2.

1 serving contains: 288 Calories (1205 kJ); 19 g Fat; 3 g Protein; 52 mg Sodium

A tall pile of toads could be called a toad-em pole.

This does double duty as a dessert and a cake.

Butter or hard margarine, softened	**2 tbsp.**	**30 mL**
Granulated sugar	**2 tbsp.**	**30 mL**
Large egg	**1**	**1**
Mild molasses	**¼ cup**	**60 mL**
Hot water	**2 tbsp.**	**30 mL**
All-purpose flour	**⅔ cup**	**150 mL**
Baking soda	**½ tsp.**	**2 mL**
Ground cinnamon	**¼ tsp.**	**1 mL**
Ground ginger	**¼ tsp.**	**1 mL**
Ground cloves	**⅛ tsp.**	**0.5 mL**
Salt	**⅛ tsp.**	**0.5 mL**
TOPPING		
Applesauce	**½ cup**	**125 mL**
Frozen whipped topping, thawed, or whipped cream (optional)	**½ cup**	**125 mL**

Place first 5 ingredients in bowl. Beat until smooth.

Add remaining 6 ingredients. Mix. Turn into greased 8 x 4 x 3 inch (20 x 10 x 7 cm) glass loaf pan. Bake in 350°F (175°C) oven for 20 to 25 minutes until an inserted wooden pick comes out clean. Cuts into 4 pieces.

Topping: Spoon applesauce over individual pieces. Top with whipped topping.

1 piece contains: 244 Calories (1021 kJ); 7.3 g Fat; 4 g Protein; 339 mg Sodium

GINGERBREAD CAKE: Simply omit topping and frost with Butter Icing, page 30.

Paré Pointer

An optimist laughs so he forgets but a pessimist forgets to laugh.

APPLE DESSERT

An easy apple dish. Browned and crunchy-looking topping.

Peeled, cored and cut up cooking apples (McIntosh is good)	2 cups	500 mL
Granulated sugar	$\frac{1}{3}$ cup	75 mL
Minute tapioca	1 tsp.	5 mL
Ground cinnamon	$\frac{1}{8}$ tsp.	0.5 mL
TOPPING		
Butter or hard margarine	2 tbsp.	30 mL
White or yellow cake mix, 1 layer size	$\frac{1}{2}$	$\frac{1}{2}$
Scoops butterscotch ripple ice cream (or vanilla)	2	2

Stir apples and sugar together in saucepan. Let stand for a few minutes until apples start to release their juices. Heat and stir to boil. Boil for 1 minute.

Add tapioca and cinnamon. Simmer, stirring occasionally, for about 5 minutes until apples are soft. Turn into ungreased 1 quart (1 L) casserole.

Topping: Melt butter in small saucepan. Stir in cake mix. Sprinkle over apple mixture. Bake, uncovered, in 350°F (175°C) oven for about 25 minutes.

Divide between 2 dishes. Top with a scoop of ice cream. Makes 2 large servings.

1 serving contains: 697 Calories (2916 kJ); 26.3 g Fat; 5 g Protein; 391 mg Sodium

Paré Pointer

About the only type of stealing that isn't dangerous is a safe robbery.

Very chocolaty. A treat for any age.

FUDGE SAUCE

Unsweetened chocolate baking square, cut up	1 × 1 oz.	1 × 28 g
Granulated sugar	¼ cup	60 mL
Skim evaporated milk	⅓ cup	75 mL
Salt, just a pinch		
Vanilla	¼ tsp.	1 mL
Ice cream scoops, vanilla or other flavor	4	4

Fudge Sauce: Combine first 5 ingredients in saucepan. Heat on low. Stir often as chocolate melts and comes almost to a boil. Remove from heat. Cool slightly. Makes ½ cup (125 mL).

Scoop ice cream into 2 dishes. Spoon warm sauce over top. It will thicken as it chills. Serves 2.

1 serving contains: 489 Calories (2045 kJ); 20.8 g Fat; 10 g Protein; 175 mg Sodium

A snap to make this luscious dessert.

Canned Bing pitted cherries, drained	14 oz.	398 mL
Semisweet chocolate chips (optional)	1 tbsp.	15 mL
Butter or hard margarine	2 tbsp.	30 mL
Chocolate cake mix, 1 layer size	½	½

Place cherries in ungreased 1 quart (1 L) casserole. Sprinkle chocolate chips over top.

Melt butter in small saucepan. Stir in ½ cake mix. Spoon over top. Pat smooth. Bake, uncovered, in 350°F (175°C) oven for 40 minutes. Divide between 2 dishes. Serves 2.

1 serving contains: 435 Calories (1715 kJ); 17.9 g Fat; 4 g Protein; 445 mg Sodium

APPLE JACK

If you like apples you will find this just so good.

Cooking apples, peeled, cored and sliced (McIntosh is good)	2	2
Granulated sugar	¼ cup	60 mL
Ground cinnamon	⅛ tsp.	0.5 mL
TOPPING		
All-purpose flour	½ cup	125 mL
Granulated sugar	¼ cup	60 mL
Cooking oil	3 tbsp.	50 mL
Baking powder	1 tsp.	5 mL
Large egg	1	1
Vanilla	½ tsp.	2 mL
Pecans, halved or chopped	2 tbsp.	30 mL

Spread apples in ungreased 1 quart (1 L) casserole. Sprinkle with sugar, then cinnamon.

Topping: Mix first 6 ingredients in bowl. Spoon over top.

Scatter pecans over top. Bake, uncovered, in 350°F (175°C) oven for about 30 minutes until apples are tender. Serves 2.

1 serving contains: 674 Calories (2819 kJ); 29 g Fat; 7 g Protein; 41 mg Sodium

1. Amber Cheesecake, page 62
2. Cream Cheese Icing, page 28
3. Carrot Cake, page 40
4. Chocolate Mosaic Cookies, page 42
5. Oatmeal Drops, page 43
6. Caramel Squares, page 145
7. Soft Molasses Cookies, page 44
8. Royal Cream Square, page 139
9. Oatmeal Chip Squares, page 141

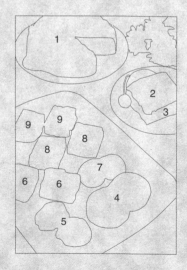

BLACK FOREST BETTY

A quick from-the-shelf dessert. Canned pie filling and cake mix. Even better with ice cream.

FILLING

Canned cherry pie filling	$\frac{1}{2}$ × 19 oz.	$\frac{1}{2}$ × 540 mL
Almond flavoring	$\frac{1}{4}$ tsp.	1 mL

TOPPING

Butter or hard margarine	2 tbsp.	30 mL
Chocolate cake mix, 1 layer size	$\frac{1}{2}$	$\frac{1}{2}$

Filling: Stir pie filling and almond flavoring together in ungreased $7\frac{3}{4}$ × $3\frac{3}{4}$ × $2\frac{1}{8}$ inch (19.5 × 9.5 × 5.5 cm) foil loaf pan. Smooth top.

Topping: Melt butter in small saucepan. Stir in cake mix until crumbly. Sprinkle over filling. Bake in 350°F (175°C) oven for about 30 minutes. Serves 2.

1 serving contains: *461 Calories (1930 kJ); 17.9 g Fat; 3 g Protein; 434 mg Sodium*

Pictured on page 71.

BROWN BETTY

Just like Mom used to make.

Cooking apples, peeled and sliced (McIntosh is good)	2	2
Granulated sugar	$\frac{1}{4}$ cup	60 mL

TOPPING

Butter or hard margarine	3 tbsp.	50 mL
Brown sugar, packed	$\frac{1}{4}$ cup	60 mL
All-purpose flour	$\frac{1}{4}$ cup	60 mL
Salt, just a pinch		

Layer apple slices with sugar in an ungreased $7\frac{3}{4}$ × $3\frac{3}{4}$ × $2\frac{1}{8}$ inch (19.5 × 9.5 × 5.5 cm) foil loaf pan.

Topping: Melt butter in saucepan. Stir in brown sugar, flour and salt. Sprinkle over apples. Pat smooth. Bake in 350°F (175°C) oven for about 30 minutes until apples are tender. Serves 2.

1 serving contains: *500 Calories (2090 kJ); 18.1 g Fat; 2 g Protein; 188 mg Sodium*

CREAM PUFFS

Baking only two cream puffs has an advantage. You can only have one.

Water	¼ cup	60 mL
Butter or hard margarine	2 tbsp.	30 mL
Salt	1/16 tsp.	0.5 mL
All-purpose flour	¼ cup	60 mL
Large egg	1	1
Whipping cream (or ¼ envelope topping)	¼ cup	60 mL
Granulated sugar	½ tsp.	2 mL
Vanilla	⅛ tsp.	0.5 mL
Icing (confectioner's) sugar, sprinkle		

Heat first 3 ingredients in small saucepan until boiling.

Add flour all at once. Stir until it forms a ball and pulls away from the sides of the pan. Remove from heat.

Add egg. Beat well. Drop by spoonfuls into 2 heaps onto greased baking sheet. Bake in 425°F (220°C) oven for about 30 minutes until they look dry. Cool.

Beat cream, sugar and vanilla in small bowl until thick. Cut tops of cream puffs almost off. Fill puffs with whipped cream. Replace tops.

Dust tops with icing sugar. Makes 2 cream puffs.

1 cream puff contains: *221 Calories (924 kJ); 15.4 g Fat; 5 g Protein; 235 mg Sodium*

Pictured on page 71.

APPETIZER PUFFS: Divide dough to make 12 tiny puffs. Bake about 20 minutes until golden brown. Cool. Fill with an appetizer spread.

Paré Pointer

A smart duck is also a wise quacker.

CHILLED CHEESECAKE

Very light in texture. Lemony and delicious. Leftovers can be frozen.

BOTTOM LAYER

Butter or hard margarine	3 tbsp.	50 mL
Graham cracker crumbs	¾ cup	175 mL
Granulated sugar	1 tbsp.	15 mL

FILLING

Envelope unflavored gelatin	1 x ¼ oz.	1 x 7 g
Water	⅓ cup	75 mL
Cream cheese, softened	8 oz.	250 g
Granulated sugar	¾ cup	175 mL
Grated peel of 1 lemon		
Juice of 1 lemon		
Milk	½ cup	125 mL
Frozen whipped topping, thawed	½ cup	125 mL

Bottom Layer: Melt butter in saucepan. Stir in graham crumbs and sugar. Pack into ungreased 7 inch (18 cm) springform pan. Set aside.

Filling: Sprinkle gelatin over water in small saucepan. Let stand 1 minute. Heat and stir until gelatin is dissolved.

Beat cream cheese, sugar, lemon peel, lemon juice and milk in bowl. Beat in gelatin mixture. Chill until mixture is thick and syrupy, stirring and scraping down sides often as it chills.

Fold in topping. Pour over bottom layer. Chill several hours. Cuts into 8 medium wedges.

1 wedge contains: 302 Calories (1265 kJ); 17.8 g Fat; 5 g Protein; 222 mg Sodium

FRUIT DIP

A smooth, yummy, beige-colored dip. A good combination with strawberries.

Sour cream	½ cup	125 mL
Brown sugar	2 tbsp.	30 mL
Grand Marnier liqueur (or other orange flavored liqueur)	1½ tsp.	7 mL

Stir all 3 ingredients together in bowl. Turn into small serving bowl in center of plate. Makes ½ cup (125 mL).

1 tbsp. (15 mL) contains: 79 Calories (329 kJ); 4.3 g Fat; 1 g Protein; 15 mg Sodium

COLLEGE PUDDING

This will remind you of a Christmas pudding but can be used any time of year.

Dry bread crumbs	1 cup	250 mL
Butter or hard margarine, melted	1/4 cup	60 mL
Raisins	1/3 cup	75 mL
Currants	1/3 cup	75 mL
Granulated sugar	1/4 cup	60 mL
Baking powder	1/2 tsp.	2 mL
Salt	1/8 tsp.	0.5 mL
Ground cinnamon	1/4 tsp.	1 mL
Ground cloves	1/16 tsp.	0.5 mL
Large eggs	2	2

Measure first 9 ingredients into bowl. Stir.

Beat eggs in separate bowl until light and volume is increased. Stir into crumb mixture. Turn into greased 3 cup (750 mL) mold. Bake in 350°F (175°C) oven for 25 to 30 minutes until an inserted wooden pick comes out clean. Serve plain or with Brown Sugar Sauce, page 131. Makes 4 smaller servings (or 2 large).

1 small serving contains: 384 Calories (1602 kJ); 10 g Fat; 8 g Protein; 461 mg Sodium

PEACH SPECIALTY

Whipped topping and candy bar crumbs over a peach gives this a real flair. A light dessert.

Large peach halves, peeled, fresh or canned, well-drained	2	2
Frozen whipped topping, thawed	1/2 cup	125 mL
Skor or Heath candy bar, finely ground or crushed	1/2	1/2

Place peach half in each dish, cut side up. Spoon whipped topping over each. Sprinkle with candy bar. Serves 2.

1 serving contains: 140 Calories (587 kJ); 6.1 g Fat; 1 g Protein; 31 mg Sodium

STRAWBERRIES SUPREME

Simple and very easy. Sauce is made from jam. Top with prepared whipped topping if desired.

RASPBERRY SAUCE

Raspberry jam	2 tbsp.	30 mL
Water	2 tbsp.	30 mL
Granulated sugar	1 tbsp.	15 mL
Lemon juice, fresh or bottled	$\frac{1}{4}$ tsp.	1 mL
Kirsch or raspberry liqueur (optional)	$\frac{1}{2}$ tsp.	2 mL
Fresh whole small strawberries or sliced large ones	1$\frac{1}{4}$ cups	300 mL
Toasted sliced almonds	1$\frac{1}{2}$ tbsp.	25 mL

Raspberry Sauce: Stir first 5 ingredients together.

Divide strawberries between 2 bowls. Spoon 2 tbsp. (30 mL) sauce over top.

Sprinkle with toasted almonds. Serves 2.

1 serving contains: *136 Calories (569 kJ); 2.9 g Fat; 2 g Protein; 4 mg Sodium*

Pictured on front cover.

RICE PUDDING

Cooking in a double boiler is best for a small rice pudding. Very good.

Short grain rice	$\frac{1}{4}$ cup	60 mL
Granulated sugar	2 tbsp.	30 mL
Milk	1 cup	250 mL
Raisins	2 tbsp.	30 mL
Salt, just a pinch		
Ground mace or cinnamon, just a pinch		
Lemon juice, fresh or bottled	$\frac{1}{8}$ tsp.	0.5 mL
Vanilla	$\frac{1}{8}$ tsp.	0.5 mL

Measure all 8 ingredients into top of double boiler. Cook over boiling water, covered, except for the times when you stir occasionally. It will take about 50 minutes for the rice to cook. Add boiling water to bottom pan as needed. Makes 1 cup (250 mL).

$\frac{1}{2}$ cup (125 mL) **contains:** *235 Calories (984 kJ); 2.7 g Fat; 6 g Protein; 66 mg Sodium*

FROZEN PEACH DESSERT

Makes a light dessert. Make ahead of time.

BOTTOM LAYER

Butter or hard margarine	4 tsp.	20 mL
Graham cracker crumbs	1/3 cup	75 mL

FILLING

Medium peach, peeled, pitted and mashed (see Note)	1	1
Granulated sugar	1 tbsp.	15 mL
Lemon juice, fresh or bottled	1/4 tsp.	1 mL
Frozen whipped topping, thawed	1/3 cup	75 mL

Bottom Layer: Melt butter in small dish. Stir in graham crumbs. Reserve 1/2 crumbs. Press remaining 1/2 in bottom of 2 fruit nappies.

Filling: Mix mashed peach, sugar and lemon juice well in bowl.

Fold in whipped topping. Spoon over crumbs in fruit nappies. Sprinkle with reserved crumbs. Freeze. Remove from freezer 20 minutes before serving. Serves 2.

1 serving contains: 316 Calories (1324 kJ); 15.1 g Fat; 4 g Protein; 366 mg Sodium

Note: To peel the peach, set in boiling water for about 30 seconds. Pull skin off using a paring knife.

CUSTARD FILLING

This makes a small amount which is very suitable for filling cream puffs or spooning over cake or gingerbread.

Milk	1/2 cup	125 mL
All-purpose flour	1 tbsp.	15 mL
Granulated sugar	1 1/2 tbsp.	25 mL
Salt	1/8 tsp.	0.5 mL
Vanilla	1/8 tsp.	0.5 mL
Large egg	1	1

Heat milk to boiling in saucepan.

Stir remaining 5 ingredients in small bowl. Stir into boiling milk until mixture returns to a boil and thickens. Cool. Makes 1/2 cup (125 mL).

1/4 cup (60 mL) contains: 126 Calories (526 kJ); 3.8 g Fat; 6 g Protein; 240 mg Sodium

Apples in pastry packets surrounded with a syrupy sauce.

SYRUP

Granulated sugar	⅔ cup	150 mL
Water	⅔ cup	150 mL
Ground cinnamon	¼ tsp.	1 mL
Ground nutmeg	¼ tsp.	1 mL
Butter or hard margarine	1 tbsp.	15 mL

APPLES

Cooking apples left whole, peeled and cored (McIntosh is good)	2	2
Brown sugar, to fill cavities	3 tbsp.	50 mL
Ground cinnamon	⅛ tsp.	0.5 mL
Butter or hard margarine	½ tsp.	2 mL

PASTRY

All-purpose flour	⅔ cup	150 mL
Baking powder	¾ tsp.	4 mL
Salt	¼ tsp.	1 mL
Solid shortening	¼ cup	60 mL
Milk	2½ tbsp.	40 mL

Syrup: Combine all 5 ingredients in saucepan. Heat and stir until mixture boils. Remove from heat.

Apples: Stuff apples with brown sugar. Divide cinnamon and butter between apples over brown sugar.

Pastry: Place first 4 ingredients in bowl. Cut in shortening until crumbly.

Add milk. Work into ball. Roll on lightly floured surface into 2 squares, 6 x 6 inch (15 x 15 cm) each. Set apple in center of each. Moisten edges. Gather pastry to top. Crimp to seal. Set apples in ungreased 1 quart (1 L) casserole. Pour in syrup. Bake, uncovered, in 375°F (190°C) oven for about 30 minutes until done. Serves 2.

1 serving contains: 894 Calories (3741 kJ); 35.3 g Fat; 6 g Protein; 431 mg Sodium

AMBER CHEESECAKE

Best served the next day. Wonderful as is but may also be topped with cherry or other pie filling. Freezes well.

BOTTOM LAYER

Butter or hard margarine	3 tbsp.	50 mL
Graham cracker crumbs	¾ cup	175 mL
Brown sugar, packed	1 tbsp.	15 mL
FILLING		
Cream cheese, softened	12 oz.	375 g
Skim evaporated milk	⅓ cup	75 mL
Brown sugar, packed	¾ cup	175 mL
All-purpose flour	1½ tbsp.	25 mL
Vanilla	1 tsp.	5 mL
Maple flavoring	¼ tsp.	1 mL
Large eggs	3	3

Bottom Layer: Melt butter in saucepan. Stir in graham crumbs and brown sugar. Pack into ungreased 7 inch (18 cm) springform pan. Bake in 350°F (175°C) oven for 10 minutes.

Filling: Combine first 6 ingredients in bowl. Beat until smooth.

Beat in eggs, 1 at a time, beating only until blended. Pour over bottom layer. Bake in 350°F (175°C) oven for 50 to 55 minutes until almost set in center. Run knife around top edge to allow cake to settle evenly. Chill. Cuts into 8 medium wedges.

1 wedge contains: 377 Calories (1576 kJ); 23.7 g Fat; 8 g Protein; 299 mg Sodium

Pictured on page 53.

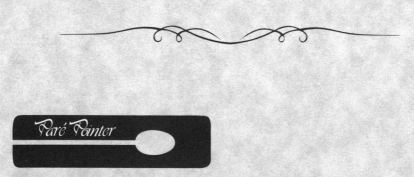

Paré Pointer

A voodoo boo boo is a witch doctor's mistake.

Worry-free dessert once this is in the freezer. Friday won't be the only day you eat this.

BOTTOM LAYER

Butter or hard margarine	$\frac{1}{3}$ cup	75 mL
Graham cracker crumbs	1$\frac{1}{2}$ cups	375 mL
Granulated sugar	2 tbsp.	30 mL
Cocoa	2 tbsp.	30 mL

FILLING

Chocolate ice cream, softened	2 cups	500 mL
Chocolate sundae topping	$\frac{1}{2}$ cup	125 mL
Strawberry ice cream, softened	2 cups	500 mL
Skor or Heath candy bar, crushed into crumbs	1	1
Chocolate sundae topping, drizzle (optional)		

Bottom Layer: Melt butter in saucepan. Stir in graham crumbs, sugar and cocoa. Reserve $\frac{1}{2}$ cup (125 mL). Press remainder in bottom of ungreased 7 inch (18 cm) springform pan.

Filling: Drop dabs of chocolate ice cream here and there over crumb layer. Spread. Sprinkle with reserved crumb mixture. Drizzle chocolate topping over crumb layer. Freeze for 10 minutes.

Spoon dabs of strawberry ice cream here and there over top. Spread. Sprinkle with candy bar crumbs. Freeze. To store, cover well.

To serve, run knife around edge, or hold hot, wet cloth around sides to loosen. Remove rim. Drizzle with chocolate sundae topping. Cut with hot knife. Makes 8 servings.

1 serving contains: 380 Calories (1588 kJ); 18.7 g Fat; 5 g Protein; 312 mg Sodium

Pictured on page 71.

Paré Pointer

According to a movie director the only way she would be in a cast was to break her leg.

BEEF NOODLE DISH

Meat and noodles in a tomato sauce. Olives show through and add to the flavor.

Cooking oil	1 tsp.	5 mL
Lean ground beef	½ lb.	227 g
Chopped onion	⅓ cup	75 mL
Chopped celery	¼ cup	60 mL
Dry medium egg noodles	1 cup	250 mL
Water	1¼ cups	300 mL
Tomato paste	½ × 5½ oz.	½ × 156 mL
Grated sharp Cheddar cheese	¼ cup	60 mL
Sliced ripe olives	¼ cup	60 mL
Beef bouillon powder	½ tsp.	2 mL
Garlic powder	¹⁄₁₆ tsp.	0.5 mL
Salt	½ tsp.	2 mL
Pepper	⅛ tsp.	0.5 mL

Heat cooking oil in frying pan. Add ground beef, onion and celery. Scramble-fry until no pink remains in beef.

Add remaining ingredients. Stir. Cover. Simmer for about 30 minutes until noodles are cooked. Makes 3 cups (750 mL).

1 cup (250 mL) contains: 310 Calories (1297 kJ); 17.9 g Fat; 20 g Protein; 761 mg Sodium

ROUND STEAK BAKE

Brown gravy, tender meat and even vegetables all in one dish.

Cooking oil	1½ tsp.	7 mL
Round or sirloin steak, cut in serving pieces	¾ lb.	340 g
Medium potatoes, quartered	2	2
Medium carrots, quartered	3	3
Medium onion, quartered	1	1
Condensed tomato soup	½ × 10 oz.	½ × 284 mL
Water	½ cup	125 mL
Salt, sprinkle		
Pepper, sprinkle		
Gravy browner, scant measure	½ tsp.	2 mL

(continued on next page)

Heat cooking oil in frying pan. Add steak pieces. Brown both sides. Transfer to ungreased 2 quart (2 L) casserole or small roaster.

Add potatoes, carrots and onion.

Combine soup, water, salt, pepper and gravy browner in bowl. Pour over top. Cover. Bake in 300°F (150°C) oven for 2¹/₂ to 3 hours until beef is tender. Serves 2 generously.

1 serving contains: 428 Calories (1789 kJ); 9.2 g Fat; 39 g Protein; 661 mg Sodium

Pictured on page 107.

Variation: Sprinkle 10 oz. (284 mL) canned green beans, drained, over top just before serving. Cover and cook about 10 minutes until beans are heated through.

HAZELNUT PERCH

A delicious dish. Tangy, crunchy, crispy and different.

Ocean perch fillets, about 5 oz. (150 g) each	2	2
All-purpose flour	2 tbsp.	30 mL
Butter or hard margarine	2 tbsp.	30 mL
HAZELNUT SAUCE		
Butter or hard margarine	1 tbsp.	15 mL
Finely chopped onion	1 tbsp.	15 mL
Sliced fresh mushrooms	¹/₂ cup	125 mL
Parsley flakes	¹/₂ tsp.	2 mL
Lemon juice, fresh or bottled	2 tbsp.	30 mL
Salt, sprinkle		
Pepper, sprinkle		
Sliced hazelnuts, toasted	2 tbsp.	30 mL

Dip fish fillets in flour to coat.

Heat butter in frying pan. Add fish. Cook, browning both sides, until fish flakes with a fork. Remove fish to plate. Keep warm.

Hazelnut Sauce: Melt butter in frying pan. Add next 6 ingredients. Stir-fry until onion and mushrooms are soft.

Stir in hazelnuts. Spoon over fish fillets. Serves 2.

1 serving contains: 385 Calories (1610 kJ); 25.1 g Fat; 30 g Protein; 293 mg Sodium

Pictured on front cover.

HAZELNUT TROUT: Use 2 pan-ready trout instead of ocean perch.

ROUND STEAK CASSEROLE

Long slow cooking produces tender meat. Rice and mushrooms cover the steak.

Hard margarine (butter browns too fast)	2 tsp.	10 mL
Round or sirloin steak, cut in serving pieces	³/₄ lb.	340 g
Chopped onion	1 cup	250 mL
Condensed cream of mushroom soup	¹/₂ × 10 oz.	¹/₂ × 284 mL
Small whole fresh mushrooms	2 cups	500 mL
Long grain white rice, uncooked	¹/₂ cup	125 mL
Water	1 cup	250 mL
Celery salt	¹/₄ tsp.	1 mL
Paprika	¹/₄ tsp.	1 mL
Pepper	¹/₈ tsp.	0.5 mL

Melt margarine in frying pan. Add steak pieces. Brown both sides well. Transfer to ungreased 2 quart (2 L) casserole.

Measure remaining 8 ingredients into frying pan. Heat and stir to loosen brown bits. Spoon over steak. Cover. Bake in 325°F (160°C) oven for 2 to 2¹/₂ hours until beef is tender. Serves 2 generously.

1 serving contains: *475 Calories (1986 kJ); 9.9 g Fat; 40 g Protein; 996 mg Sodium*

SLOPPY JOES

Slightly tangy, slightly sweet. This makes an easy meal. Serve over split and buttered hamburger buns.

Cooking oil	1 tsp.	5 mL
Lean ground beef	1 lb.	454 g
Chopped onion	¹/₂ cup	125 mL
Chopped green pepper	¹/₄ cup	60 mL
Condensed tomato soup	¹/₂ × 10 oz.	¹/₂ × 284 mL
Ketchup	¹/₄ cup	60 mL
Water	2 tbsp.	30 mL
White vinegar	1¹/₂ tbsp.	25 mL
Brown sugar	1¹/₂ tbsp.	25 mL
Worcestershire sauce	¹/₂ tsp.	2 mL
Water, to thin mixture	2-4 tbsp.	30-60 mL

(continued on next page)

Heat cooking oil in frying pan. Add ground beef, onion and green pepper. Scramble-fry until beef is browned.

Add next 6 ingredients. Stir. Simmer, covered, for about 20 minutes.

Stir in enough water to make a slightly runny mixture if needed. Makes 2 cups (500 mL).

½ cup (125 mL) contains: 332 Calories (1390 kJ); 18.9 g Fat; 22 g Protein; 561 mg Sodium

CHICKEN IN SAUCE

Cubes of chicken match the small whole mushrooms. A creamy looking dish. Serve with rice or noodles.

Boneless, skinless chicken breast halves	**½ lb.**	**227 g**
Water, to cover		
Small whole fresh mushrooms	**⅔ cup**	**150 mL**
Butter or hard margarine	**1½ tbsp.**	**25 mL**
All-purpose flour	**1½ tbsp.**	**25 mL**
Chicken bouillon powder	**1 tsp.**	**5 mL**
Milk	**½ cup**	**125 mL**
Skim evaporated milk	**¼ cup**	**60 mL**
Salt	**⅛ tsp.**	**0.5 mL**
Pepper	**⅛ tsp.**	**0.5 mL**
Sherry (or alcohol-free sherry)	**1 tsp.**	**5 mL**
Slivered pimiento	**1 tbsp.**	**15 mL**

Cover chicken with water in saucepan. Boil for 8 to 10 minutes until tender. Do not drain. Remove chicken. Chop. Place in bowl.

Add mushrooms to chicken broth. Cook for about 3 minutes until soft. Drain. Add to chicken.

Melt butter in saucepan. Mix in flour and bouillon powder. Stir in both milks, salt and pepper until mixture boils and thickens. Add chicken and mushrooms. Add more salt if needed. Remove from heat.

Stir in sherry and pimiento. Serves 2.

1 serving contains: 313 Calories (1309 kJ); 13 g Fat; 33 g Protein; 748 mg Sodium

POT ROAST

Appearance is wonderful and unusual. A dark brown gravy with a hint of tomato and carrot showing through.

Cooking oil	1 tsp.	5 mL
Beef chuck or blade roast, bone-in	1½ lbs.	680 g
Boiling water	½ cup	125 mL
All-purpose flour	1½ tbsp.	25 mL
Water	¼ cup	60 mL
Canned tomatoes, with juice, mashed	½ cup	125 mL
Finely chopped onion	1 tbsp.	15 mL
Medium carrot, sliced	1	1
Salad dressing (or mayonnaise)	1 tbsp.	15 mL
Ketchup	1 tbsp.	15 mL
Salt, sprinkle		
Pepper, sprinkle		

Heat cooking oil in heavy saucepan. Brown beef roast on both sides.

Add first amount of water. Simmer for 2 to 2½ hours until tender. Add more water if needed. Remove roast to plate. Cover to keep warm.

Mix flour and second amount of water in small bowl until smooth. Stir into liquid in saucepan. Heat and stir to boil and thicken.

Add remaining ingredients. Simmer, covered, until onion and carrot are cooked. Serve with roast. Makes 2 servings.

1 serving contains: 439 Calories (1838 kJ); 21.7 g Fat; 44 g Protein; 342 mg Sodium

BAKED SOLE

A carefree way to cook fish. Just sauce it and bake it.

Sole fillets, about 6 oz. (170 g) each	2	2
Fresh medium mushrooms, sliced	3	3
Sour cream	1½ tbsp.	25 mL
Salad dressing (or mayonnaise)	1½ tbsp.	25 mL
Lemon juice, fresh or bottled	1 tsp.	5 mL
Onion powder, just a pinch		

(continued on next page)

Lay fish fillets side by side in 9 inch (22 cm) pie plate. Scatter mushroom slices over top.

Mix sour cream, salad dressing, lemon juice and onion powder in small bowl. Spread over all. Bake, uncovered, in 350°F (175°C) oven for about 20 minutes until fish flakes with fork. Serves 2.

1 serving contains: 242 Calories (1013 kJ); 9.9 g Fat; 33 g Protein; 222 mg Sodium

SPAGHETTI TUNA CASSEROLE

A bit zesty with cheese, pimiento and green peppers added.

PASTA		
Spaghetti	¼ lb.	113 g
Boiling water	2 qts.	2 L
Cooking oil (optional)	2 tsp.	10 mL
Salt (optional)	2 tsp.	10 mL
SAUCE		
Butter or hard margarine	2 tbsp.	30 mL
All-purpose flour	2 tbsp.	30 mL
Salt	⅛ tsp.	0.5 mL
Milk	1 cup	250 mL
Grated medium or sharp Cheddar cheese	⅔ cup	150 mL
Condensed tomato soup	½ × 10 oz.	½ × 284 mL
Finely chopped onion	⅓ cup	75 mL
Finely chopped green pepper	¼ cup	60 mL
Pimiento slivers (optional)	1 tbsp.	15 mL
Canned flaked tuna, drained	6½ oz.	184 g

Pasta: Cook spaghetti in boiling water, cooking oil and salt in large uncovered saucepan for 11 to 13 minutes until tender but firm. Drain.

Sauce: Melt butter in separate saucepan. Mix in flour and salt. Stir in milk until boiling and thickened.

Add cheese. Stir to melt.

Add remaining 5 ingredients and spaghetti. Stir. Turn into ungreased 1 quart (1 L) casserole. Cover. Bake in 350°F (175°C) oven for 30 minutes. Remove cover. Bake for 10 minutes. Makes 3 cups (750 mL).

1 cup (250 mL) contains: 501 Calories (2097 kJ); 20 g Fat; 34 g Protein; 783 mg Sodium

OMELET

Start the day with a colorful omelet.

Large eggs	**4**	**4**
Water	**2 tbsp.**	**30 mL**
Salt, sprinkle		
Pepper, sprinkle		
FILLING		
Diced cooked ham	**¼ cup**	**60 mL**
Grated medium Cheddar cheese	**¼ cup**	**60 mL**
Diced seeded tomato (optional)	**2 tbsp.**	**30 mL**
Chopped green onion (optional)	**2 tbsp.**	**30 mL**
Diced mushrooms (optional)	**2 tbsp.**	**30 mL**
Grated medium Cheddar cheese	**1-2 tbsp.**	**15-30 mL**

Beat eggs, water, salt and pepper together in bowl until smooth. Pour into greased non-stick 10 inch (25 cm) frying pan heated to medium-low. Cover. Cook without stirring until almost set.

Filling: Sprinkle with first 5 ingredients. Cover. Cook until set. Fold in half. Remove to plate.

Sprinkle second amount of cheese over top. Divide to serve 2.

*¹/₂ **omelet contains:** 330 Calories (1379 kJ); 23.8 g Fat; 26 g Protein; 609 mg Sodium*

1. Raisin Pie, page 111
2. Swiss Mocha, page 11
3. Cream Puffs, page 56
4. Black Forest Betty, page 55
5. Frosty Friday, page 63

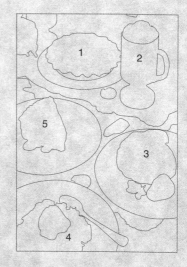

Deep and delicious.

PIZZA CRUST

All-purpose flour	1½ cups	375 mL
Envelope instant yeast (1½ tsp., 7 mL)	½ × ¼ oz.	½ × 8 g
Granulated sugar	1 tsp.	5 mL
Baking powder	1 tsp.	5 mL
Cooking oil	1½ tbsp.	25 mL
Warm water	⅔ cup	150 mL

PIZZA SAUCE

Tomato sauce	7½ oz.	213 mL
All-purpose flour	2 tbsp.	30 mL
Whole oregano	¾ tsp.	4 mL
Granulated sugar	½ tsp.	2 mL
Dried sweet basil	¼ tsp.	1 mL
Salt	¼ tsp.	1 mL
Pepper	⅛ tsp.	0.5 mL
Garlic powder	⅛ tsp.	0.5 mL
Ground thyme	⅛ tsp.	0.5 mL

TOPPING

Grated Monterey Jack cheese	½ cup	125 mL
Lean ground beef, scramble-fried and drained (or sliced pepperoni)	¼ lb.	113 g
Sliced fresh mushrooms	1 cup	250 mL
Green onion, sliced	1	1
Slivered red pepper	¼ cup	60 mL
Grated mozzarella cheese (add more if desired)	½ cup	125 mL

Pizza Crust: Stir first 4 ingredients together in bowl.

Add cooking oil and warm water. Stir well. Turn out onto floured surface. Knead 30 to 40 times until smooth and elastic. A food processor can do this kneading for you. Grease 9 inch (22 cm) glass pie plate. (If you are really a pizza lover, use a 12 inch, 30 cm pizza pan and add a bit more topping.) Roll and stretch, fitting dough into pie plate and pressing dough part way up sides.

Pizza Sauce: Stir tomato sauce gradually into flour in saucepan so no lumps remain. Measure in next 7 ingredients. Heat, stirring often, until sauce simmers and thickens. Cool. Spread over crust.

Topping: Sprinkle Monterey Jack cheese over sauce followed by ground beef or pepperoni, mushrooms, green onion and red pepper. Top with mozzarella cheese. Bake in 400°F (205°C) oven for 15 to 18 minutes. Cuts into 8 wedges.

1 wedge contains: 286 Calories (1197 kJ); 11.5 g Fat; 13 g Protein; 670 mg Sodium

Pictured on page 89.

SPAGHETTI AND MEATBALLS

A meal in itself. A salad or a vegetable could be added.

SPAGHETTI SAUCE

Canned tomatoes, with juice, mashed	1 cup	250 mL
Ketchup	1/4 cup	60 mL
Chopped onion	1/3 cup	75 mL
Parsley flakes	1/2 tsp.	2 mL
Dried sweet basil	1/4 tsp.	1 mL
Whole oregano	1/4 tsp.	1 mL
Granulated sugar	1/2 tsp.	2 mL
Salt	1/8 tsp.	0.5 mL
Pepper	1/8 tsp.	0.5 mL

MEATBALLS

Water	2 tbsp.	30 mL
Dry bread crumbs	1/4 cup	60 mL
Dry onion flakes	1 tsp.	5 mL
Whole oregano	1/8 tsp.	0.5 mL
Garlic powder	1/8 tsp.	0.5 mL
Grated Parmesan cheese	2 tsp.	10 mL
Salt, sprinkle		
Pepper, sprinkle		
Lean ground beef	1/2 lb.	227 g
Cooking oil	2 tsp.	10 mL

PASTA

Spaghetti	4 oz.	125 g
Boiling water	2 qts.	2 L
Cooking oil (optional)	1 tsp.	5 mL
Salt (optional)	1 tsp.	5 mL
Grated Parmesan cheese, sprinkle		

Spaghetti Sauce: Combine all 9 ingredients in saucepan. Bring to a simmer. Cover. Simmer for about 30 minutes. If too runny, cook, uncovered, to thicken.

Meatballs: Mix water, bread crumbs, onion flakes, oregano, garlic powder, cheese, salt and pepper in bowl.

Add ground beef. Mix well. Shape into 1 1/2 inch (3.5 cm) balls.

Heat cooking oil in frying pan. Add meatballs. Turn often or better yet shake pan often to keep balls round. Cook until no pink remains in beef.

Pasta: Cook spaghetti in boiling water, cooking oil and salt in large uncovered saucepan for 11 to 13 minutes until tender but firm. Drain. Divide onto 2 plates. Top with meatballs. Spoon sauce over top.

Sprinkle with Parmesan cheese. Serves 2.

1 serving contains: 665 Calories (2783 kJ); 24.4 g Fat; 34 g Protein; 1040 mg Sodium

Pictured on page 89.

Well-suited for a romantic dinner for two.

STUFFING

Hard margarine (butter browns too fast)	**2 tsp.**	**10 mL**
Chopped onion	**¼ cup**	**60 mL**
Chopped celery	**¼ cup**	**60 mL**
Small bread cubes	**1½ cups**	**375 mL**
Salt, scant measure	**¼ tsp.**	**1 mL**
Pepper	**¹⁄₁₆ tsp.**	**0.5 mL**
Poultry seasoning, generous measure	**¼ tsp.**	**1 mL**
Chicken bouillon powder	**½ tsp.**	**2 mL**
Applesauce	**⅓ cup**	**75 mL**
Cornish hen, about 1 lb. (454 g) **(see Note)**	**1**	**1**
Applesauce, for glazing	**¼ cup**	**60 mL**

Stuffing: Melt margarine in frying pan. Add onion and celery. Sauté until tender-crisp. Remove from heat.

Add bread cubes, salt, pepper, poultry seasoning, bouillon powder and first amount of applesauce. Stir. Add more applesauce if needed. Stuffing should hold together when a handful is squeezed.

Spread stuffing in bottom of small roaster. Lay Cornish hen halves, cut side down, over stuffing. Cover. Bake in 375°F (190°C) oven for 45 to 60 minutes.

Remove cover. Brush with remaining applesauce. Continue to bake, uncovered, for 15 to 20 minutes until tender and glazed. Remove to dish. Keep warm.

1 serving contains: 416 Calories (1740 kJ); 24.7 g Fat; 24 g Protein; 773 mg Sodium

Note: Have your butcher or meat department personnel cut frozen hen in half down the middle. Thaw just before baking.

BEEF ROULADE

A "jelly roll" meat filled with a tasty mixture. Serve in attractive slices.

Round steak, cut ¼ inch (6 mm) thick, or pound thicker steak until ¼ inch (6 mm) thick	¾ lb.	340 g
Prepared mustard	2 tsp.	10 mL
Salt, sprinkle		
Pepper, sprinkle		
Finely chopped onion	¼ cup	60 mL
Bacon slices, cooked and diced	3	3
Chopped pimiento	1 tbsp.	15 mL
Chopped dill pickle	2 tbsp.	30 mL
All-purpose flour	1 tbsp.	15 mL
Hard margarine (butter browns too fast)	2 tsp.	10 mL
Boiling water	1 cup	250 mL
Beef bouillon powder	1½ tsp.	7 mL
Red wine (or alcohol-free red wine)	¼ cup	60 mL
Medium onion, quartered	1	1

Lay steak on counter.

Spread with next 7 ingredients in order given. Roll up and tie with string.

Coat meat roll with flour. Melt margarine in frying pan. Add meat roll. Brown quickly and well. Set in ungreased small casserole.

Pour boiling water over beef bouillon powder in small bowl. Stir. Add red wine and onion. Stir. Pour over meat roll. Cover. Bake in 325°F (160°C) oven for about 1½ hours until tender. Slice before serving. Serves 2.

1 serving contains: 353 Calories (1477 kJ); 13.5 g Fat; 39 g Protein; 792 mg Sodium

Variation: Instead of baking, roll may be simmered, covered, for same length of time until tender. Meat will be much darker in appearance.

BROCCOLI HAM STRATA

A make-ahead that is yellow with ham bits showing through. Excellent taste.

White bread slices, crusts removed	2½-3	2½-3
Grated sharp Cheddar cheese	⅓ cup	75 mL
Frozen chopped broccoli, thawed and drained	½ × 10 oz.	½ × 284 mL
Cooked ham slices, diced	3	3
Large eggs	2	2
Milk	¾ cup	175 mL
Dry onion flakes	1½ tsp.	7 mL
Salt	⅛ tsp.	0.5 mL
Dry mustard powder	1/16 tsp.	0.5 mL

Layer bread, cheese, broccoli and ham in greased 9 × 5 × 3 inch (22 × 12 × 7 cm) aluminum loaf pan.

Beat eggs in bowl. Add milk, onion flakes, salt and mustard powder. Beat in. Pour over all. Cover. Refrigerate overnight. Remove cover. Bake in 325°F (160°C) oven for 45 to 55 minutes until set. Let stand 5 minutes before cutting. Serves 2.

1 serving contains: 364 Calories (1522 kJ); 19.3 g Fat; 26 g Protein; 1217 mg Sodium

Pictured on page 89.

ROAST IN GRAVY

Flavored with onion. This is a super easy and fast way to prepare meat and gravy.

Lean boneless beef roast, such as sirloin tip	1½ lbs.	680 g
Condensed cream of mushroom soup	½ × 10 oz.	½ × 284 mL
Envelope dry onion soup mix (stir before dividing)	½ × 1½ oz.	½ × 42 g
Water	¼ cup	60 mL

Lay roast on long piece of foil in small roaster.

Stir soup, onion soup mix and water together in small bowl. Pour over meat. Fold foil edges together. Cover roaster. Bake in 300°F (150°C) oven for 1½ to 2 hours until desired degree of doneness. After removing meat to platter, pour gravy into bowl to serve. Serves 4, or 2 generously.

1 small serving contains: 281 Calories (1174 kJ); 15.6 g Fat; 30 g Protein; 420 mg Sodium

SALISBURY STEAK

Serve these with a sauce for the ultimate flavor. Use pan drippings to make Savory Sauce, page 97.

Dry bread crumbs	$\frac{1}{3}$ cup	75 mL
Salt	$\frac{1}{2}$ tsp.	2 mL
Pepper	$\frac{1}{8}$ tsp.	0.5 mL
Finely minced onion	2 tbsp.	30 mL
Milk	$\frac{1}{3}$ cup	75 mL
Soy sauce	2 tsp.	10 mL
Beef bouillon powder	1 tsp.	5 mL
Lean ground beef	1 lb.	454 g

Measure bread crumbs, salt, pepper, onion, milk, soy sauce and bouillon powder into bowl. Stir.

Add ground beef. Mix well. Shape into 4 small oval patties $\frac{3}{4}$ inch (2 cm) thick. Broil 8 to 10 minutes per side until browned and cooked through. Makes 4 "steaks".

1 patty contains: 299 Calories (1251 kJ); 18 g Fat; 24 g Protein; 818 mg Sodium

CORNED BEEF CASSEROLE

Adding the macaroni raw makes this a convenient from-the-shelf dish. A real time saver.

Dry elbow macaroni	$1\frac{1}{2}$ cups	375 mL
Canned corned beef, crumbled in small chunks	$\frac{1}{2} \times 12$ oz.	$\frac{1}{2} \times 340$ g
Chopped onion	$\frac{1}{2}$ cup	125 mL
Grated sharp Cheddar cheese	$\frac{1}{4}$ cup	60 mL
Condensed cream of chicken soup	$\frac{1}{2} \times 10$ oz.	$\frac{1}{2} \times 284$ mL
Milk	$1\frac{1}{2}$ cups	375 mL

Stir all 6 ingredients together in ungreased $1\frac{1}{2}$ quart (1.5 L) casserole. Cover. Bake in 350°F (175°C) oven for about 50 minutes, stirring at half time. Makes 4 cups (1 L).

1 cup (250 mL) contains: 382 Calories (1598 kJ); 13.6 g Fat; 23 g Protein; 822 mg Sodium

BEEFY RICE

Actually a frying pan casserole. Very easy. Add a salad to complete the meal.

Cooking oil	1 tbsp.	15 mL
Lean ground beef	½ lb.	227 g
Chopped onion	⅓ cup	75 mL
Chopped celery	¼ cup	60 mL
Grated carrot	¼ cup	60 mL
Sliced fresh mushrooms	½ cup	125 mL
Boiling water	1½ cups	375 mL
Instant rice	1½ cups	375 mL
Beef bouillon powder	2 tsp.	10 mL
Soy sauce	2 tbsp.	30 mL
Salt, sprinkle		

Heat cooking oil in frying pan. Add ground beef, onion, celery, carrot and mushrooms. Sauté until no pink remains in beef and vegetables are soft.

Add remaining 5 ingredients. Stir. Cover. Simmer slowly for 1 to 2 minutes. Makes 4 cups (1 L).

1 cup (250 mL) contains: 317 Calories (1325 kJ); 12.3 g Fat; 15 g Protein; 869 mg Sodium

TACO MEATBALLS

These may be used as an appetizer as well as a main course.

Large egg	1	1
Dry taco seasoning mix (stir before measuring)	2 tbsp.	30 mL
Dry bread crumbs	2 tbsp.	30 mL
Lean ground beef	½ lb.	227 g

Beat egg in bowl. Mix in taco seasoning and bread crumbs.

Add ground beef. Mix well. Shape into 1 tbsp. (15 mL) size balls. Arrange in shallow baking pan in single layer. Bake in 375°F (190°C) oven for about 15 minutes. Makes 21 meatballs.

1 meatball contains: 30 Calories (127 kJ); 1.9 g Fat; 2 g Protein; 15 mg Sodium

SPAGHETTI AND SAUCE

Excellent flavors. Dark brown with a red sauce.

SPAGHETTI MEAT SAUCE

Cooking oil	2 tsp.	10 mL
Lean ground beef	1/2 lb.	227 g
Chopped onion	1/3 cup	75 mL
Chopped green pepper	2 tbsp.	30 mL
Sliced fresh mushrooms	2/3 cup	150 mL
Canned tomatoes, with juice, cut up	1/2 cup	125 mL
Ketchup	1/4 cup	60 mL
Red wine (or alcohol-free red wine)	2 tbsp.	30 mL
Small bay leaf	1	1
Worcestershire sauce	1/2 tsp.	2 mL
Celery salt	1/8 tsp.	0.5 mL
Garlic powder	1/8 tsp.	0.5 mL
Salt, sprinkle		

PASTA

Spaghetti	4 oz.	125 g
Boiling water	2 qts.	2 L
Cooking oil (optional)	1 tsp.	5 mL
Salt (optional)	1 tsp.	5 mL

Grated Parmesan cheese, sprinkle

Spaghetti Meat Sauce: Heat cooking oil in frying pan. Add ground beef, onion, green pepper and mushrooms. Scramble-fry until no pink remains in beef.

Add next 8 ingredients. Stir. Cook gently, stirring often, for 10 minutes. Add a bit of water if it gets too dry.

Pasta: Cook spaghetti in boiling water, cooking oil and salt in large uncovered saucepan for 11 to 13 minutes until tender but firm. Drain. Serve with sauce mixed in or in a separate bowl.

Sprinkle with Parmesan cheese. Serves 2.

1 serving contains: 597 Calories (2496 kJ); 23 g Fat; 31 g Protein; 628 mg Sodium

A tasty red sauce makes a great finishing touch.

STOCK

Chopped onion	⅓ cup	75 mL
Chopped celery	¼ cup	60 mL
Small bay leaf	1	1
Grated carrot	⅓ cup	75 mL
White vinegar	1½ tbsp.	25 mL
Salt	⅛ tsp.	0.5 mL
Pepper, sprinkle		
Water	1 cup	250 mL

TOMATO SAUCE

Canned tomatoes, with juice, broken up	1 cup	250 mL
Chopped onion	½ cup	125 mL
Garlic powder	¼ tsp.	1 mL
Whole oregano	⅛ tsp.	0.5 mL
Granulated sugar	¼ tsp.	1 mL
Salt, sprinkle		
Pepper, sprinkle		
Apple juice (or prepared orange juice)	1 tbsp.	15 mL
Salmon fillets or steaks, about 6 oz. (170 g) each	2	2

Stock: Combine first 8 ingredients in saucepan. Bring to a boil. Cook for 10 minutes until vegetables are tender.

Tomato Sauce: Measure first 8 ingredients into blender. Process until onion is puréed. Pour into separate saucepan. Heat to simmer. Continue to simmer for about 3 minutes to cook onion.

Add salmon to carrot mixture. Simmer for about 10 minutes until salmon flakes when tested with a fork. Remove salmon with slotted spoon to warm plates. Discard stock. Spoon Tomato Sauce over top of salmon. Makes 2 servings.

1 serving contains: 290 Calories (1212 kJ); 11.2 g Fat; 35 g Protein; 283 mg Sodium

Pictured on page 143.

Paré Pointer

An odd thing happened when she saw a goat in the creamery. It turned to butt-'er.

PORK CHOP BAKE

Deep brown in color. This is a very satisfying way of serving chops.

Hard margarine (butter browns too fast)	2 tsp.	10 mL
Loin pork chops, trimmed of fat	2	2
Chopped onion	1 cup	250 mL
All-purpose flour	1 tsp.	5 mL
Salt, sprinkle		
Pepper, sprinkle		
Apple juice	1/2 cup	125 mL
Soy sauce	1-2 tsp.	5-10 mL

Melt margarine in frying pan. Add pork chops. Add onion to edge of pan, away from chops. Brown chops on both sides and stir onions occasionally as they brown. Transfer chops to greased 1 quart (1 L) casserole.

Sprinkle onion with flour, salt and pepper. Mix.

Stir in apple juice and desired amount of soy sauce until sauce boils and thickens. Pour over pork chops. Cover. Bake in 350°F (175°C) oven for about 1¼ hours until pork is tender. Serves 2.

1 serving contains: 254 Calories (1064 kJ); 12.2 g Fat; 19 g Protein; 322 mg Sodium

OVEN BEEF STEW

Your meal-in-one waiting in the oven.

Stewing beef, trimmed of fat, cut bite size	1/2 lb.	227 g
Medium-small potatoes, cut bite size	2	2
Medium carrots, cut bite size	2	2
Medium onion, cut bite size	1	1
Sliced celery	1/2 cup	125 mL
Canned tomatoes, with juice, mashed	14 oz.	398 mL
Granulated sugar	2 tsp.	10 mL
Beef bouillon powder	2 tsp.	10 mL
Prepared horseradish	1 tsp.	5 mL
Salt	1/2 tsp.	2 mL
Pepper	1/8 tsp.	0.5 mL
Water	1/3 cup	75 mL

(continued on next page)

Place beef in ungreased 2 quart (2 L) casserole or in small roaster. Add vegetables.

Combine remaining 7 ingredients in bowl. Stir well. Pour over beef. Cover. Bake in 300°F (150°C) oven for about 3¼ to 3½ hours until beef is very tender. Makes 4½ cups (1.1 L). Serves 2.

1 serving contains: 322 Calories (1348 kJ); 4.6 g Fat; 24 g Protein; 1704 mg Sodium

Pictured on page 89.

MUSHROOM SAUCED PASTA

A simple pleasant pasta dish.

MUSHROOM SAUCE

Butter or hard margarine	1 tbsp.	15 mL
Chopped onion	⅓ cup	75 mL
Tiny whole mushrooms or sliced larger mushrooms	2 cups	500 mL
Salt, sprinkle		
Pepper, sprinkle		
Sour cream	¼ cup	60 mL

PASTA

Broad egg noodles	1 cup	250 mL
Boiling water	2 qts.	2 L
Cooking oil (optional)	2 tsp.	10 mL
Salt	2 tsp.	10 mL

Mushroom Sauce: Melt butter in frying pan. Add onion. Sauté until soft.

Add mushrooms. Sauté until moisture has cooked away and mushrooms are soft.

Sprinkle with salt and pepper. Add sour cream. Stir. Keep warm. Makes ⅔ cup (150 mL) sauce.

Pasta: Cook noodles in boiling water, cooking oil and salt in large uncovered saucepan for 5 to 7 minutes until tender but firm. Drain. Turn noodles into bowl. Pour sauce over top. Stir gently. Serves 2.

1 serving contains: 204 Calories (853 kJ); 11.3 g Fat; 6 g Protein; 81 mg Sodium

MEATBALLS

Dark and glossy, these are baked with a great sauce.

Large egg	1	1
Finely chopped onion	3 tbsp.	50 mL
Salt	$\frac{1}{2}$ tsp.	2 mL
Pepper	$\frac{1}{8}$ tsp.	0.5 mL
Dry bread crumbs	$\frac{1}{3}$ cup	75 mL
Lean ground beef	6 oz.	170 g
SAUCE		
Barbecue sauce (regular)	$\frac{1}{4}$ cup	60 mL
Apricot jam	$\frac{1}{3}$ cup	75 mL

Stir egg, onion, salt and pepper together in bowl. Add bread crumbs. Stir.

Add ground beef. Mix. If too soft, add a touch more crumbs. Shape into 1 inch (2.5 cm) balls. Arrange on broiler pan. Broil for about 10 minutes each side or bake in 350°F (175°C) oven for 15 minutes. Turn into ungreased 8 × 8 inch (20 × 20 cm) pan.

Sauce: Measure barbecue sauce and jam into small bowl. Stir. Spoon over meatballs in pan being sure to get some on every one. Bake, uncovered, for about 30 minutes. Makes 13 meatballs.

1 meatball contains: 74 Calories (308 kJ); 2.6 g Fat; 3 g Protein; 182 mg Sodium

COUNTRY STYLE CHICKEN

Make this when you can get tiny mushrooms. Has a colorful sauce.

Hard margarine (butter browns too fast)	1 tbsp.	15 mL
Chicken parts, skin removed	4	4
(2 thighs and 2 breast halves)		
Chopped onion	$\frac{1}{3}$ cup	75 mL
All-purpose flour	2 tsp.	10 mL
Chicken bouillon powder	$\frac{1}{2}$ tsp.	2 mL
Salt, sprinkle		
Pepper, sprinkle		
Canned tomatoes, with juice, mashed	1 cup	250 mL
Small whole fresh mushrooms	1 cup	250 mL

(continued on next page)

Melt margarine in frying pan. Add chicken. Brown both sides. Remove to plate.

Add onion to pan. Sauté until soft.

Mix in flour, bouillon powder, salt and pepper. Stir in tomatoes and mushrooms until mixture boils. Add chicken. Cover. Simmer for 40 to 45 minutes until tender. Serves 2.

1 serving contains: *362 Calories (1514 kJ); 14.5 g Fat; 44 g Protein; 544 mg Sodium*

CREAMY CRAB

A flavorful creamy mixture. Serve with noodles, rice or potatoes.

Hard margarine (butter browns too fast)	1 tbsp.	15 mL
Chopped onion	¼ cup	60 mL
Chopped fresh mushrooms	½ cup	125 mL
All-purpose flour	4 tsp.	20 mL
Chicken bouillon powder	¼ tsp.	1 mL
Cayenne pepper, just a pinch		
Salt, sprinkle		
Skim evaporated milk	1¼ cups	300 mL
Chopped pimiento	2 tsp.	10 mL
Canned crabmeat, drained (or 1 cup, 250 mL fresh, cooked), membrane removed	4 oz.	113 g

Melt margarine in frying pan. Add onion and mushrooms. Sauté until soft.

Mix in flour, bouillon powder, cayenne and salt. Stir in milk until mixture boils and thickens.

Add pimiento and crabmeat. Stir. Heat through. Serves 2.

1 serving contains: *261 Calories (1090 kJ); 6.7 g Fat; 23 g Protein; 744 mg Sodium*

SPANISH MEATLOAF

A loaf with lots of flavor.

Large egg	1	1
Ketchup	3 tbsp.	50 mL
Finely chopped onion	2 tbsp.	30 mL
Finely chopped celery	1 tbsp.	15 mL
Dry bread crumbs	¼ cup	60 mL
Lemon juice, fresh or bottled	1 tbsp.	15 mL
Chili powder	1 tsp.	5 mL
Whole oregano	¼ tsp.	1 mL
Garlic powder	⅛ tsp.	0.5 mL
Salt, sprinkle		
Pepper, sprinkle		
Lean ground beef	¾ lb.	340 g
Ketchup	1 tbsp.	15 mL

Mix first 11 ingredients in bowl.

Add ground beef. Mix well. Shape into loaf on ungreased double foil. Bring up sides to enclose. Leave top open. Place in open shallow pan. Bake in 350°F (175°C) oven for 45 minutes.

Spread second amount of ketchup over top. Continue baking for 15 minutes. Serves 2.

1 serving contains: *508 Calories (2126 kJ); 29.2 g Fat; 38 g Protein; 678 mg Sodium*

FETTUCCINE ALFREDO

Try this delicious, low-fat version. Serve a green salad with this pasta treat and you're all set.

Fettuccine	8 oz.	250 g
Boiling water	2½ qts.	2.5 L
Cooking oil (optional)	2 tsp.	10 mL
Salt (optional)	2 tsp.	10 mL
Skim evaporated milk	¾ cup	175 mL
Grated Parmesan cheese	¼ cup	60 mL
Salt	¼ tsp.	1 mL
Pepper	⅛ tsp.	0.5 mL

(continued on next page)

Cook fettuccine in boiling water, cooking oil and salt in large uncovered pot for 5 to 7 minutes until tender but firm. Drain. Return fettuccine to pot.

Combine milk, cheese, salt and pepper in separate saucepan. Heat, stirring constantly, until almost boiling. Cheese should no longer be granular. Stir into pasta. Serves 2.

1 serving contains: 604 Calories (2527 kJ); 6.2 g Fat; 29 g Protein; 713 mg Sodium

FRIED CHICKEN

An old favorite served with a milk gravy.

All-purpose flour	**3 tbsp.**	**50 mL**
Seasoned salt	**$3/4$ tsp.**	**4 mL**
Pepper	**$1/8$ tsp.**	**0.5 mL**
Cooking oil	**2 tbsp.**	**30 mL**
Chicken parts, skin removed, about $1^1/4$ lbs. (560 g)	**4-6**	**4-6**
MILK GRAVY		
All-purpose flour	**$1^1/2$ tbsp.**	**25 mL**
Paprika	**$1/8$ tsp.**	**0.5 mL**
Salt	**$1/4$ tsp.**	**1 mL**
Pepper	**$1/16$ tsp.**	**0.5 mL**
Milk	**$3/4$ cup**	**175 mL**

Stir flour, seasoned salt and pepper together in bowl.

Heat cooking oil in frying pan. Dip chicken parts in flour mixture. Brown well in hot cooking oil. Cover. Cook slowly for about 30 minutes, turning occasionally, until tender. Transfer chicken to dish. Keep warm.

Milk Gravy: Stir flour into pan juices. If there are no juices, melt $1^1/2$ tbsp. (25 mL) butter or hard margarine with the flour. Mix in salt, pepper and paprika. Stir in milk until mixture boils and thickens. Be sure to loosen brown bits in pan. Add a bit more milk if gravy is too thick. Serve with chicken. Serves 2.

1 serving contains: 452 Calories (1892 kJ); 20.1 g Fat; 46 g Protein; 524 mg Sodium

BEEF SHORT RIBS

A wonderful way to serve short ribs. Potatoes and carrots can be added or not, as you like.

Beef short ribs, trimmed of fat	1½ lbs.	680 g
Finely chopped onion	¼ cup	60 mL
Envelope dry onion soup mix (stir before dividing)	½ × 1½ oz.	½ × 42 g
Condensed tomato soup	½ × 10 oz.	½ × 284 mL
Mild molasses	1 tbsp.	15 mL
White vinegar	1 tbsp.	15 mL
Medium potatoes, quartered	2	2
Medium carrots, slice in 1 inch (2.5 cm) lengths	4	4

Arrange short ribs in small roaster.

Mix next 5 ingredients in bowl. Spoon over short ribs. Cover. Bake in 300°F (150°C) oven for 3 hours. Tilt roaster so juice runs to end. Spoon off fat.

Add potatoes and carrots. Cover. Continue to bake for about 1 hour until meat and vegetables are tender. Serves 2.

1 serving contains: 579 Calories (2423 kJ); 19.8 g Fat; 40 g Protein; 1593 mg Sodium

1. Oven Beef Stew, page 82
2. Broccoli Ham Strata, page 77
3. Spaghetti And Meatballs, page 74
4. Pizza Deluxe, page 73

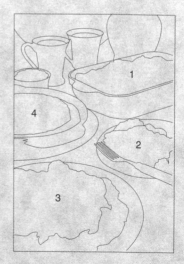

Serving Dishes And Glassware Courtesy Of:
The Bay China Dept.

Dinner And Side Plates Courtesy Of:
Creations By Design

A mild cheese-flavored dish with a bit of color from the ketchup.

Cooking oil	1 tsp.	5 mL
Lean ground beef	1/2 lb.	225 g
Cream cheese, softened	1/2 × 4 oz.	1/2 × 125 g
Ketchup	1/3 cup	75 mL
Creamed cottage cheese	3/4 cup	175 mL
Milk	1/3 cup	75 mL
Parsley flakes	1 tsp.	5 mL
Onion powder	1/2 tsp.	2 mL
Salt, sprinkle		

PASTA

Fusilli (about 1 1/4 cups, 300 mL)	4 oz.	125 g
Boiling water	2 qts.	2 L
Cooking oil (optional)	2 tsp.	10 mL
Salt (optional)	2 tsp.	10 mL

Heat cooking oil in frying pan. Add ground beef. Scramble-fry until browned. Drain off any fat.

Beat cream cheese, ketchup and cottage cheese in bowl. Add milk, parsley, onion powder and salt. Beat to mix. Stir in ground beef.

Pasta: Cook fusilli in boiling water, cooking oil and salt in large uncovered saucepan for 8 to 10 minutes until tender but firm. Drain. Layer 1/2 fusilli in greased 7 3/4 × 3 3/4 × 2 1/8 inch (19.5 × 9.5 × 5.5 cm) foil loaf pan, 1/2 meat sauce, 1/2 fusilli and 1/2 meat sauce. Bake, uncovered, in 350°F (175°C) oven for about 30 minutes. Cover and bake for 15 minutes more. Serves 2.

1 serving contains: 455 Calories (1903 kJ); 25.2 g Fat; 37 g Protein; 1089 mg Sodium

Pare Pointer

Cows caught in earthquakes give great milk shakes.

T.V. BUNWICHES

A super treat. A natural for watching the game on television. Hot bread stuffed with beef.

Cooking oil	½ tsp.	2 mL
Lean ground beef	¼ lb.	113 g
Chopped onion	2 tbsp.	30 mL
Frozen chopped spinach, thawed	¼ × 10 oz.	¼ × 300 g
Lemon juice, fresh or bottled	¾ tsp.	4 mL
Ground nutmeg, just a pinch		
Salt, sprinkle		
Pepper, sprinkle		
Frozen bread buns, 2 oz. (56 g) size, thawed	6	6

Heat cooking oil in frying pan. Add ground beef and onion. Scramble-fry until no pink remains in meat. Drain well.

Add next 5 ingredients. Scramble-fry to cook spinach.

Roll 1½ buns into 4 × 4 inch (10 × 10 cm) square. Put 2 tbsp. (30 mL) beef mixture in center. Dampen corners. Bring up 4 corners to meet in center. Pinch corners together. Arrange on greased baking sheet. Repeat. Cover with greased waxed paper and tea towel. Let stand in oven with light on and door closed for about 45 minutes. Remove from oven. Heat oven to 350°F (175°C). Bake bunwiches for about 25 minutes. Makes 4.

1 bunwich contains: 297 Calories (1317 kJ); 10.9 g Fat; 12 g Protein; 445 mg Sodium

Variation: Brush the warm tops with ½ tsp. (2 mL) butter.

Pictured on page 107.

Paré Pointer

A witch's favorite breakfast is scrambled hex.

Such an appetizing appearance with a reddish tinge from the addition of ketchup.

All-purpose flour	**2 tbsp.**	**30 mL**
Seasoned salt	**$\frac{1}{8}$ tsp.**	**0.5 mL**
Pepper	**$\frac{1}{16}$ tsp.**	**0.5 mL**
Hard margarine (butter browns too fast)	**1 tbsp.**	**15 mL**
Minute steaks (tenderized round steak) about 6 oz. (170 g) each	**2**	**2**
Butter or hard margarine	**1 tbsp.**	**15 mL**
All-purpose flour	**1 tbsp.**	**15 mL**
Water	**$\frac{1}{2}$ cup**	**125 mL**
Ketchup	**$\frac{1}{4}$ cup**	**60 mL**
Medium onion, cut in chunks	**1**	**1**

Mix first amount of flour, seasoned salt and pepper in shallow bowl.

Melt margarine in fairly hot frying pan. Dip steaks in flour mixture to coat. Add to pan. Quickly brown both sides. Transfer to ungreased 1 quart (1 L) casserole.

Melt butter in frying pan. Mix in second amount of flour. Stir in water and ketchup until mixture boils and thickens. Remove from heat.

Scatter onion around steaks. Pour sauce over all. Cover. Bake in 325°F (160°C) oven for 1 to 1$\frac{1}{2}$ hours until steaks are tender. Serves 2.

1 serving contains: 377 Calories (1577 kJ); 15.7 g Fat; 35 g Protein; 627 mg Sodium

ROUND SWISS STEAK: Omit minute steak. Use $\frac{3}{4}$ lb. (340 g) round steak, about $\frac{1}{2}$ inch (12 mm) thick. Oven cooking time may be a bit longer. Serves 2.

Paré Pointer

Oak trees make acorns. Tight shoes make corns ache.

SAUCED RIBS

Zippy ribs. Sauced and oven baked.

Chili sauce or ketchup	⅓ cup	75 mL
Water	2 tbsp.	30 mL
Brown sugar	1½ tbsp.	25 mL
Worcestershire sauce	1 tbsp.	15 mL
Prepared mustard	1 tbsp.	15 mL
Beef bouillon powder	2 tsp.	10 mL
Salt, sprinkle		
Pepper, sprinkle		
Pork spareribs, cut in 2 or 3 rib pieces	1¼ lb.	570 g

Stir first 8 ingredients together in small bowl.

Coat each section of ribs with mixture and place in small roaster. Spoon remaining sauce, if any, over top. Cover. Bake in 350°F (175°C) oven for about 1½ hours until tender. Makes 2 servings.

1 serving contains: *610 Calories (2551 kJ); 38.9 g Fat; 39 g Protein; 1492 mg Sodium*

SNAPPY STROGANOFF

Use for a meal or a snack. Good served with rice, noodles or potatoes.

Cooking oil	1 tsp.	5 mL
Lean ground beef	½ lb.	227 g
Finely chopped onion	⅓ cup	75 mL
Sliced fresh mushrooms (or canned, drained)	½ cup	125 mL
All-purpose flour	1 tbsp.	15 mL
Beef bouillon powder	1 tsp.	5 mL
Paprika	¼ tsp.	1 mL
Salt, sprinkle		
Pepper,sprinkle		
Canned cream of chicken soup	½ × 10 oz.	½ × 284 mL
Low-fat sour cream (7% MF), or regular	¼ cup	60 mL

(continued on next page)

Heat cooking oil in frying pan or saucepan. Add ground beef, onion and mushrooms. Scramble-fry until no pink remains in beef and onion is soft. Do not drain.

Sprinkle with flour, bouillon powder, paprika, salt and pepper. Mix well. Add soup. Stir until mixture boils and thickens.

Stir in sour cream. Heat through. Serves 2.

1 serving contains: *395 Calories (1653 kJ); 26.2 g Fat; 25 g Protein; 977 mg Sodium*

SHEPHERD'S PIE

So tasty. A favorite for sure.

Cooking oil	**1 tsp.**	**5 mL**
Lean ground beef	**½ lb.**	**227 g**
Chopped onion	**1¼ cups**	**300 mL**
Water	**⅓ cup**	**75 mL**
Beef bouillon powder	**2 tsp.**	**10 mL**
Medium carrot, diced or very thinly sliced	**1**	**1**
Garlic powder	**⅛ tsp.**	**0.5 mL**
Worcestershire sauce	**¼ tsp.**	**1 mL**
Salt, sprinkle		
Pepper, sprinkle		
Frozen peas	**⅓ cup**	**75 mL**
Cooked mashed potatoes	**1½ cups**	**375 mL**
Milk	**1 tbsp.**	**15 mL**
Salt, sprinkle		
Paprika, sprinkle		

Heat cooking oil in frying pan. Add ground beef and onion. Scramble-fry until beef is browned and onion is soft. Drain.

Combine next 7 ingredients in saucepan. Stir. Heat to boiling. Cook slowly until carrot is tender.

Add peas. Cook for 2 to 3 minutes. Add ground beef mixture. Stir. Pack into 7¹⁵/₁₆ x 5⁷/₁₆ x 1⁷/₈ inch (20.2 x 13.8 x 4.7 cm) foil freezer carton.

Cover with mashed potato. Sprinkle with paprika. Bake, uncovered, in 350°F (175°C) oven for about 30 minutes until very hot. Serves 2.

1 serving contains: *426 Calories (1784 kJ); 12.5 g Fat; 27 g Protein; 686 mg Sodium*

CORNED BEEF PASTA

Good tomato flavor. Pasta is added raw which makes it very convenient.

Dry elbow macaroni	1$\frac{1}{2}$ cups	375 mL
Canned tomatoes, with juice, mashed	14 oz.	398 mL
Canned corned beef, crumbled	$\frac{1}{2}$ x 12 oz.	$\frac{1}{2}$ x 340 g
in small chunks		
Tomato juice	1 cup	250 mL
Milk	2 tbsp.	30 mL
TOPPING		
Butter or hard margarine	1 tbsp.	15 mL
Cracker crumbs	$\frac{1}{4}$ cup	60 mL

Measure first 5 ingredients into ungreased 1$\frac{1}{2}$ quart (1.5 L) casserole. Cover. Bake in 350°F (175°C) oven for about 40 minutes to cook macaroni. Stir before adding topping.

Topping: Melt butter in small saucepan. Add cracker crumbs. Stir well. Sprinkle over top. Return, uncovered, to oven. Bake for about 10 minutes. Makes 4 cups (1 L).

1 cup (250 mL) contains: 344 Calories (1440 kJ); 11 g Fat; 19 g Protein; 913 mg Sodium

COQ AU VIN

This excellent variation contains no bacon. Out of the ordinary to be sure.

Hard margarine (butter browns too fast)	1 tbsp.	15 mL
Chicken parts, skin removed (about	4-5	4-5
1$\frac{1}{4}$ lbs., 560 g)		
All-purpose flour	$\frac{1}{4}$ cup	60 mL
Sliced onion	$\frac{1}{2}$ cup	125 mL
Canned tomatoes, with juice, mashed	14 oz.	398 mL
Small whole fresh mushrooms	2 cups	500 mL
Bay leaf	1	1
Garlic powder	$\frac{1}{8}$ tsp.	0.5 mL
Granulated sugar	$\frac{1}{4}$ tsp.	1 mL
Salt, sprinkle		
Pepper, sprinkle		
Red wine (or alcohol-free red wine)	$\frac{1}{4}$ cup	60 mL

(continued on next page)

Melt margarine in frying pan. Dip chicken in flour. Add and brown both sides. Transfer to ungreased 1½ quart (1.5 L) casserole.

Add onion to pan. Sauté until browned.

Add next 7 ingredients to onion. Stir. Cover. Cook slowly for 5 minutes. Discard bay leaf.

Stir in wine. Pour over chicken. Cover. Bake in 325°F (160°C) oven for 1 to 1½ hours until tender. Serves 2.

1 serving contains: 422 Calories (1767 kJ); 10.8 g Fat; 47 g Protein; 537 mg Sodium

Pictured on page 17.

PEPPER STEAK

Wonderful flavor with a delicious sauce.

Whole peppercorns	**1 tbsp.**	**15 mL**
Boneless sirloin steaks, about 6 oz. (170 g) each, trimmed of fat	**2**	**2**
Cooking oil	**1 tbsp.**	**15 mL**
SAVORY SAUCE		
Butter or hard margarine	**1 tbsp.**	**15 mL**
All-purpose flour	**1 tbsp.**	**15 mL**
Salt	**½ tsp.**	**2 mL**
Apple juice	**½ cup**	**125 mL**
Skim evaporated milk	**1 cup**	**250 mL**
Chopped green onion	**2 tsp.**	**10 mL**

Crush peppercorns between 2 sheets of waxed paper with hammer. Sprinkle ½ over one side of steaks. Press into beef with heel of hand. Repeat with other side.

Heat cooking oil in frying pan. Add steaks. Brown and cook to desired doneness. Remove to plate. Keep warm.

Savory Sauce: Melt butter in frying pan. Mix in flour and salt. Stir in apple juice, milk and green onion. Heat and stir until mixture boils and thickens, being sure to loosen any brown bits in pan. Pour over steaks. Serves 2.

1 serving contains: 467 Calories (1955 kJ); 19.4 g Fat; 45 g Protein; 969 mg Sodium

OVEN FRIED CHICKEN

Enjoy deep-fried taste without the deep-frying.

Fine dry bread crumbs	$1/3$ cup	75 mL
Grated Parmesan cheese	2 tbsp.	30 mL
Salt	$1/4$ tsp.	1 mL
Paprika	$1/8$ tsp.	0.5 mL
Seasoned salt	$1/4$ tsp.	1 mL
Chicken parts, skin removed, about $1^{1}/_{4}$ lbs. (560 g)	4-6	4-6

Combine first 5 ingredients in plastic bag. Mix well.

Add 2 pieces of chicken at a time. Shake to coat. Arrange in single layer on broiler pan or greased foil-lined pan. Bake in 350°F (175°C) oven for about 1 hour until tender. Serves 2.

1 serving contains: *317 Calories (1325 kJ); 7 g Fat; 46 g Protein; 734 mg Sodium*

Pictured on page 125.

BAKED STEAK

A dark reddish-brown appearance. Double recipe for a good company dish.

All-purpose flour	1 tbsp.	15 mL
Salt	$1/4$ tsp.	1 mL
Pepper	$1/8$ tsp.	0.5 mL
Sirloin steak, cut in serving pieces	$3/4$ lb.	340 g
Cooking oil	1 tbsp.	15 mL
Condensed tomato soup	$1/2 \times 10$ oz.	$1/2 \times 284$ mL
Chopped onion	$1/4$ cup	60 mL
Brown sugar	1 tbsp.	15 mL
Lemon juice, fresh or bottled	1 tsp.	5 mL
Prepared mustard	$1/2$ tsp.	2 mL
Worcestershire sauce	2 tsp.	10 mL
Garlic powder	$1/8$ tsp.	0.5 mL
Celery salt	$1/8$ tsp.	0.5 mL
Water	$1/4$ cup	60 mL

(continued on next page)

Mix flour, salt and pepper in small bowl.

Lay steak on working surface. Sprinkle flour mixture over one side at a time, pounding into each side.

Heat cooking oil in frying pan. Brown steak on both sides. Transfer to ungreased 1 quart (1 L) casserole.

Mix remaining 9 ingredients in bowl. Pour over steak. Cover. Bake in 325°F (160°C) oven for 1 to 1½ hours until steak is tender. Serves 2.

1 serving contains: 369 Calories (1542 kJ); 14.4 g Fat; 36 g Protein; 1026 mg Sodium

CHICKEN STROGANOFF

This creamy dish goes well with rice or noodles. Quick stove-top chicken.

Cooking oil	1 tbsp.	15 mL
Boneless, skinless chicken breast halves, cut in cubes or strips	2	2
Chopped onion	⅓ cup	75 mL
Sliced fresh mushrooms	1 cup	250 mL
All-purpose flour	2 tsp.	10 mL
Salt, generous measure	¼ tsp.	1 mL
Pepper	¹⁄₁₆ tsp.	0.5 mL
Thyme	¹⁄₁₆ tsp.	0.5 mL
Paprika	⅛ tsp.	0.5 mL
Water	½ cup	125 mL
Low-fat sour cream (7% MF), or regular	½ cup	125 mL
Sherry (or alcohol-free sherry), optional	2-3 tsp.	10-15 mL

Heat cooking oil in frying pan. Add chicken and onion. Stir-fry for about 5 minutes to brown and cook.

Add mushrooms. Stir-fry for 2 minutes more.

Mix in flour, salt, pepper, thyme and paprika. Stir in water and sour cream until mixture boils and thickens slightly.

Stir in sherry. Serves 2.

1 serving contains: 279 Calories (1167 kJ); 12.9 g Fat; 31 g Protein; 445 mg Sodium

HONEY CHICKEN

So quick and easy. Simply pour a sauce over chicken and bake. Soy sauce is a natural with chicken. Lots of sauce to serve over rice or potatoes.

Chicken thighs, skin removed	1¼ lbs.	570 g
Honey	¼ cup	60 mL
Soy sauce	2 tbsp.	30 mL
Ketchup	2 tsp.	10 mL
Salt, sprinkle		
Pepper, sprinkle		

Arrange chicken pieces in single layer in ungreased 2 quart (2 L) casserole.

Mix remaining ingredients in bowl. Pour over chicken. Cover. Bake in 350°F (175°C) oven for 1 to 1½ hours until tender. Serves 2.

1 serving contains: 341 Calories (1428 kJ); 6.2 g Fat; 33 g Protein; 1252 mg Sodium

TUNA CASSEROLE

A complete meal in one dish. Good eating.

Broad noodles	2 cups	500 mL
Boiling water	2 qts.	2 L
Cooking oil (optional)	2 tsp.	10 mL
Salt (optional)	1 tsp.	5 mL
Hard margarine (butter browns too fast)	2 tsp.	10 mL
Chopped onion	½ cup	125 mL
All-purpose flour	1 tbsp.	15 mL
Salt, sprinkle		
Pepper, sprinkle		
Milk	1 cup	250 mL
Canned flaked tuna, drained	6½ oz.	184 g
Cooked peas, fresh or frozen	⅔ cup	150 mL
Coarsely crushed corn flakes (or grated medium or sharp Cheddar cheese)	¼ cup	60 mL

(continued on next page)

Cook noodles in boiling water, cooking oil and first amount of salt in large uncovered saucepan for 5 to 7 minutes until tender but firm. Drain. Return noodles to saucepan.

Melt margarine in separate saucepan. Add onion. Sauté until soft.

Mix in flour, second amount of salt and pepper. Stir in milk until boiling and thickened.

Add tuna, peas and noodles. Stir. Turn into ungreased 2 quart (2 L) casserole.

Sprinkle with corn flakes crumbs. Bake, uncovered, in 350°F (175°C) oven for about 25 minutes. Serves 2.

1 serving contains: *497 Calories (2081 kJ); 8.7 g Fat; 42 g Protein; 618 mg Sodium*

FISH CAKES

Nicely browned patties. A good use for leftover fish.

Cooked, mashed potatoes	1½ cups	375 mL
Shredded or mashed cooked fish	½ cup	125 mL
Large egg	1	1
Onion powder	¼ tsp.	1 mL
Salt	½ tsp.	2 mL
Pepper	⅛ tsp.	0.5 mL
Parsley flakes	¼ tsp.	1 mL
Fine dry bread crumbs	¼ cup	60 mL
Hard margarine (butter browns too fast)	2 tsp.	10 mL

Mix first 8 ingredients in order given in bowl. Divide into 4 equal portions. Shape each portion into ¾ inch (2 cm) thick patty.

Melt margarine in frying pan. Add fish cakes. Brown both sides. Serves 2.

1 serving contains: *372 Calories (1558 kJ); 8.2 g Fat; 25 g Protein; 940 mg Sodium*

Pictured on page 107.

BOSTON BLUE BROIL

Fish fillets give better results when broiling if they are the same thickness.

Cooking oil	2 tsp.	10 mL
Salad dressing (or mayonnaise)	2 tbsp.	30 mL
Grated Parmesan cheese	2 tbsp.	30 mL
Chopped chives	1 tbsp.	15 mL
Lemon juice, fresh or bottled	2 tsp.	10 mL
Boston bluefish fillets	12 oz.	375 g
Lemon juice, fresh or bottled	2 tsp.	10 mL
Salt, sprinkle		
Pepper, sprinkle		

Stir first 5 ingredients together in small bowl.

Lay a piece of foil on broiler pan. Arrange fish fillets over foil. Drizzle with second amount of lemon juice. Sprinkle with salt and pepper. Broil 4 to 5 inches (10 to 12.5 cm) from heat for about 4 minutes until fish flakes when tested with fork. Spoon cheese mixture over fish. Broil for 4 to 5 minutes to brown. Serves 2.

1 serving contains: *379 Calories (1585 kJ); 21.8 g Fat; 40 g Protein; 324 mg Sodium*

MUSTARD SAUCED CHICKEN

You will probably wish you had doubled this recipe. It is superb.

Boneless, skinless chicken breasts, halved	½ lb.	227 g
All-purpose flour	1 tbsp.	15 mL
Hard margarine (butter browns too fast)	1 tbsp.	15 mL
All-purpose flour	2 tsp.	10 mL
Chicken bouillon powder	1½ tsp.	7 mL
Water	⅓ cup	75 mL
Skim evaporated milk	⅔ cup	150 mL
Prepared mustard	½ tsp.	2 mL
Prepared horseradish	½ tsp.	2 mL
Sliced fresh mushrooms	½ cup	125 mL

(continued on next page)

Dip chicken into first amount of flour to coat. Melt margarine in frying pan. Add chicken. Brown both sides. Transfer to ungreased 1 quart (1 L) casserole or smaller.

Add second amount of flour and bouillon powder to frying pan. Add a bit more margarine if needed to moisten flour. Stir in water, milk, mustard and horseradish. Heat and stir until mixture boils and thickens.

Stir in mushrooms. Pour over chicken. Cover. Bake in 325°F (160°C) oven for 1 to 1½ hours until tender. Serves 2.

1 serving contains: 288 Calories (1203 kJ); 7.8 g Fat; 36 g Protein; 753 mg Sodium

Pictured on page 107.

CHICKEN SIMPLISTIC

A great in-a-hurry recipe. The tarragon gives this a bit of a different flavor.

Chicken parts, skin removed (about 1¼ lbs., 560 g)	**4-5**	**4-5**
Condensed onion soup	½ × 10 oz.	½ × 284 mL
White vinegar	½ tsp.	2 mL
Garlic powder	⅛ tsp.	0.5 mL
Tarragon leaves, finely crushed	⅛ tsp.	0.5 mL
Skim evaporated milk (or light cream)	2 tbsp.	30 mL
Cornstarch	2 tsp.	10 mL
Water	1 tbsp.	15 mL

Arrange chicken in single layer, meaty side down, in ungreased 2 quart (2 L) casserole.

Stir next 5 ingredients together in small bowl. Pour over chicken. Cover. Bake in 350°F (175°C) oven for 1 to 1½ hours until tender. Transfer chicken to bowl. Keep warm.

Stir cornstarch into water. Mix into juice in casserole. Boil in microwave to thicken or if using a metal pan, heat and stir to boiling on burner. Serves 2.

1 serving contains: 270 Calories (1129 kJ); 5.3 g Fat; 44 g Protein; 790 mg Sodium

SHRIMP STRATA

A simply scrumptious make-ahead.

Bread slices, cut in 1 inch (2.5 cm) squares	2	2
Grated sharp Cheddar cheese	1/2 cup	125 mL
Canned shrimp, drained, rinsed and drained again (or 1 cup, 250 mL fresh, cooked)	4 oz.	113 g
Large egg	1	1
Milk	2/3 cup	150 mL
Dry mustard powder	1/8 tsp.	0.5 mL
Salt	1/8 tsp.	0.5 mL

Put bread squares, cheese and shrimp into bowl. Toss. Place in greased 1 quart (1 L) casserole.

Beat egg in small bowl. Add milk, mustard powder and salt. Beat. Pour over shrimp mixture. Cover. Let stand overnight in refrigerator. Remove cover. Bake in 350°F (175°C) oven for about 45 minutes. Serves 2.

1 serving contains: *324 Calories (1357 kJ); 16 g Fat; 27 g Protein; 634 mg Sodium*

SUKIYAKI

This tastes as good as it looks. Different from the usual fare.

Cooking oil	1 tbsp.	15 mL
Sirloin steak, sliced in paper thin strips	6 oz.	170 g
Diagonally sliced celery	3/4 cup	175 mL
Coarsely chopped onion	1 cup	250 mL
Chopped fresh mushrooms	1 cup	250 mL
Canned sliced water chestnuts, drained	8 oz.	227 mL
Canned bamboo shoots, drained	8 oz.	227 mL
Cornstarch	2 tsp.	10 mL
Water	1/2 cup	125 mL
Soy sauce	1/4 cup	60 mL
Granulated sugar	1 1/2 tbsp.	25 mL
Beef bouillon powder	1 tsp.	5 mL

(continued on next page)

Heat cooking oil in frying pan. Add steak strips. Brown quickly, stirring, for about 5 minutes. Remove strips to bowl.

Place next 5 ingredients in frying pan. Stir-fry slowly for about 5 minutes until tender, adding more cooking oil if needed.

Stir cornstarch into water in cup. Add soy sauce, sugar and bouillon powder. Add to vegetables. Stir to boil and thicken. Add beef. Stir. Heat through. Serves 2.

1 serving contains: 335 Calories (1400 kJ); 10.8 g Fat; 24 g Protein; 2582 mg Sodium

Pictured on page 107.

BLUEBERRY PIE

Good warm or cold. Serve plain or with whipped topping or ice cream.

Granulated sugar	¼ cup	60 mL
All-purpose flour	1 tbsp.	15 mL
Salt	¹⁄₁₆ tsp.	0.5 mL
Blueberries, fresh or frozen	1 cup	250 mL
Pastry, page 114, enough for double crust 6 inch (15 cm) pie		
Granulated sugar, sprinkle (optional)		

Stir first amount of sugar, flour and salt together in medium bowl.

Add blueberries. Toss well.

Roll out bottom crust and line 6 inch (15 cm) foil pie plate. Fill with blueberry mixture. Roll out top crust. Moisten bottom edge. Cover with pastry. Trim. Crimp to seal. Cut a few slits in top.

Sprinkle with remaining sugar. Bake in 350°F (175°C) oven for 40 to 45 minutes until browned. Cuts into 4 small wedges.

1 wedge contains: 282 Calories (1179 kJ); 13.9 g Fat; 3 g Protein; 129 mg Sodium

COTTAGE PIE

Very much like a custard pie. To make it special, top with a dash of red jam or jelly preserves.

Granulated sugar	¼ cup	60 mL
All-purpose flour	1½ tsp.	7 mL
Creamed cottage cheese, sieved or smoothed in blender	½ cup	125 mL
Large egg	1	1
Skim evaporated milk (or light cream)	¼ cup	60 mL
Vanilla	¼ tsp.	1 mL
Salt, just a pinch		
Unbaked 6 inch (15 cm) pie shell, page 114	1	1

Stir sugar and flour together in bowl.

Add cottage cheese. Beat in egg. Add milk, vanilla and salt. Stir.

Pour into pie shell. Bake in 350°F (175°C) oven for about 35 minutes. Cuts into 4 small wedges.

1 wedge contains: 215 Calories (899 kJ); 8.8 g Fat; 8 g Protein; 200 mg Sodium

1. Fish Cakes, page 101
2. Round Steak Bake, page 64
3. T.V. Bunwiches, page 92
4. Mustard Sauced Chicken, page 102
5. Sukiyaki, page 104

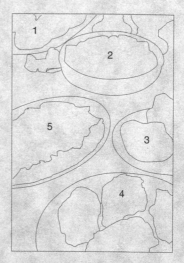

Tablecloth Courtesy Of:
La Cache

Place Mat / Mugs Courtesy Of:
Le Gnome

Serving Dishes Courtesy Of:
Enchanted Kitchen

Meringue topped and absolutely delicious.

Granulated sugar	3 tbsp.	50 mL
All-purpose flour	2 tbsp.	30 mL
Egg yolk (large)	1	1
Ground cinnamon	¼ tsp.	1 mL
Ground allspice	⅛ tsp.	0.5 mL
Ground cloves, just a pinch		
Sour cream	½ cup	125 mL
Raisins	¼ cup	60 mL
Baked 6 inch (15 cm) pie shell, page 114	1	1
MERINGUE		
Egg white (large), room temperature	1	1
Cream of tartar	⅛ tsp.	0.5 mL
Granulated sugar	2 tbsp.	30 mL

Mix sugar and flour in bowl. Stir in egg yolk. Add cinnamon, allspice, cloves, sour cream and raisins. Mix well. Heat and stir until mixture comes to a boil and thickens. Cool until you can hold your hand on saucepan.

Pour into pie shell.

Meringue: Beat egg white and cream of tartar together in small bowl until fairly stiff. Gradually beat in sugar until very stiff. Spoon over pie, sealing to edge. Bake in 350°F (175°C) oven for about 10 minutes until golden brown. Cuts into 4 small wedges.

1 wedge contains: 271 Calories (1134 kJ); 12.5 g Fat; 4 g Protein; 85 mg Sodium

GINGERSNAP CRUST

Use for cooked fillings. It adds a different flavor to a plain custard.

Butter or hard margarine	1½ tbsp.	25 mL
Finely crushed gingersnaps	⅓ cup	75 mL
Granulated sugar	1 tsp.	5 mL

Melt butter in small saucepan. Stir in crumbs and sugar. Press into bottom and up sides of 6 inch (15 cm) foil pie plate. Bake in 350°F (175°C) oven for 5 minutes. Cool. Makes 1 small crust.

¼ crust contains: 97 Calories (408 kJ); 5.9 g Fat; 1 g Protein; 118 mg Sodium

SWEET POTATO PIE

Similar to pumpkin pie. Serve with whipped cream or frozen whipped topping, thawed.

Large egg	1	1
Granulated sugar	1/4 cup	60 mL
Ground cinnamon	1/4 tsp.	1 mL
Ground ginger	1/8 tsp.	0.5 mL
Ground nutmeg	1/8 tsp.	0.5 mL
Salt	1/16 tsp.	0.5 mL
Cooked, mashed sweet potatoes	1/3 cup	75 mL
Skim evaporated milk	1/3 cup	75 mL
Unbaked 6 inch (15 cm) pie shell, page 114	1	1

Beat egg in small bowl. Add next 6 ingredients. Beat.

Mix in milk.

Pour into pie shell. Bake in 400°F (205°C) oven for 10 minutes. Reduce heat. Continue to bake in 350°F (175°C) oven for about 30 minutes. If you insert a knife just off center, it should come out quite clean. Cuts into 4 small wedges.

1 wedge contains: 219 Calories (918 kJ); 8.3 g Fat; 5 g Protein; 95 mg Sodium

APPLE PIE

Your favorite pie in miniature. Serve warm or cold. Add cheese slices and/or ice cream.

Pastry, page 114, enough for 2 crust, 6 inch (15 cm) pie		
Granulated sugar	1/4 cup	60 mL
All-purpose flour	1 1/2 tsp.	7 mL
Ground cinnamon	1/8 tsp.	0.5 mL
Salt	1/16 tsp.	0.5 mL
Peeled, cored and cut up cooking apples (McIntosh is good)	1 1/4 cups	300 mL
Granulated sugar, sprinkle (optional)		

(continued on next page)

Roll out pastry and fit bottom crust in 6 inch (15 cm) foil pie plate.

Stir first amount of sugar, flour, cinnamon and salt together in medium bowl.

Add apple. Toss well. Turn into pie shell. Roll out crust for top. Moisten bottom edges. Position top crust. Trim. Crimp to seal. Cut a few slits in top.

Sprinkle with remaining sugar. Bake in 350°F (175°C) oven for about 40 minutes until apples are tender. Cuts into 4 small wedges.

1 wedge contains: 277 Calories (1160 kJ); 13.9 g Fat; 2 g Protein; 93 mg Sodium

RAISIN PIE

Still a favorite, this must have been one of the first pies to grace the table.

Raisins	**1 cup**	**250 mL**
Water	**$1/3$ cup**	**75 mL**
Lemon juice, fresh or bottled	**2 tsp.**	**10 mL**
Prepared orange juice	**2 tbsp.**	**30 mL**
Brown sugar, packed	**$1/3$ cup**	**75 mL**
All-purpose flour	**2 tsp.**	**10 mL**
Salt	**$1/8$ tsp.**	**0.5 mL**

Pastry, page 114, enough for double crust 6 inch (15 cm) pie

Granulated sugar, sprinkle (optional)

Heat first 4 ingredients in saucepan, stirring often, until boiling.

Mix brown sugar, flour and salt in small bowl. Stir into boiling mixture until it returns to a boil and thickens. Cool thoroughly. Set saucepan in cold water to hasten cooling.

Roll out bottom crust and line 6 inch (15 cm) foil pie plate. Turn raisin filling into shell. Roll out top crust. Moisten bottom edge. Put on top crust. Trim. Crimp to seal. Cut slits in top.

Sprinkle with sugar. Bake in 400°F (205°C) oven for about 25 minutes until browned. Cuts into 4 small wedges.

1 wedge contains: 384 Calories (1608 kJ); 14 g Fat; 3 g Protein; 185 mg Sodium

Pictured on page 71.

BUTTERSCOTCH PIE

A rich taste to this meringue topped pie.

Water	³/₄ cup	175 mL
Butter or hard margarine	1 tsp.	5 mL
Brown sugar, packed	¹/₂ cup	125 mL
All-purpose flour	¹/₄ cup	60 mL
Salt	¹/₈ tsp.	0.5 mL
Egg yolk (large)	1	1
Water	2 tbsp.	30 mL
Vanilla	¹/₂ tsp.	2 mL
Baked 6 inch (15 cm) pie shell, page 114	1	1
MERINGUE		
Egg white (large), room temperature	1	1
Cream of tartar	¹/₈ tsp.	0.5 mL
Granulated sugar	2 tbsp.	30 mL

Heat first amount of water and butter in saucepan to boiling.

Stir brown sugar, flour and salt together in small bowl.

Mix in egg yolk, second amount of water and vanilla. Stir until mixture returns to a boil and thickens.

Pour into pie shell.

Meringue: Beat egg white and cream of tartar together in small bowl until almost stiff. Gradually beat in sugar until stiff. Pile on pie sealing to edge. Bake in 350°F (175°C) oven for about 10 minutes until golden brown. Cuts into 4 small wedges.

1 wedge contains: 293 Calories (1227 kJ); 9.2 g Fat; 4 g Protein; 177 mg Sodium

Paré Pointer

Batteries get sick too from acid indigestion.

A perfect size. Smooth creamy filling topped with meringue.

GRAHAM CRACKER CRUST

Butter or hard margarine	1½ tbsp.	25 mL
Graham cracker crumbs	⅓ cup	75 mL
Granulated sugar	1 tsp.	5 mL

CUSTARD FILLING

Milk	⅔ cup	150 mL
All-purpose flour	3 tbsp.	50 mL
Granulated sugar	3 tbsp.	50 mL
Salt	⅛ tsp.	0.5 mL
Vanilla	¼ tsp.	1 mL
Egg yolk (large)	1	1
Milk	2 tbsp.	30 mL

MERINGUE

Egg white (large), room temperature	1	1
Cream of tartar	⅛ tsp.	0.5 mL
Granulated sugar	2 tbsp.	30 mL
Reserved crumb mixture	1 tsp.	5 mL

Graham Cracker Crust: Melt butter in small saucepan. Stir in graham crumbs and sugar. Reserve 1 tsp. (5 mL). Press the rest in bottom and up sides of 6 inch (15 cm) foil pie plate. Bake in 350°F (175°C) oven for 5 minutes. Cool.

Custard Filling: Heat first amount of milk until boiling.

Stir flour, sugar and salt together in small bowl. Mix in vanilla, egg yolk and second amount of milk. Stir into boiling milk until mixture returns to a boil and thickens. Cool 10 minutes. Pour into pie shell.

Meringue: Beat egg white and cream of tartar together in small bowl until almost stiff. Gradually beat in sugar until stiff. Spread over pie, sealing to edge.

Sprinkle with reserved crumbs. Bake in 350°F (175°C) oven for 10 minutes until golden. Cuts into 4 small wedges.

1 wedge contains: 211 Calories (882 kJ); 8.1 g Fat; 5 g Protein; 254 mg Sodium

PASTRY

This makes a small quantity which makes it easy to make your own pie crusts.

All-purpose flour	1¼ cups	300 mL
Brown sugar	2 tsp.	10 mL
Baking powder	¼ tsp.	1 mL
Salt	¼ tsp.	1 mL
Lard (or shortening)	½ cup	125 mL
Cold water	3 tbsp.	50 mL

Measure first 4 ingredients into bowl. Cut in lard until crumbly.

Sprinkle with water. Stir with fork. Shape into a ball. If necessary, a small amount of extra water may be added, about 1 tsp. (5 mL) at a time if needed. The less water used, the better. Makes enough for 4, 6 inch (15 cm) single crust pies or 2, 6 inch (15 cm) double crust pies.

1 single crust contains: 404 Calories (1691 kJ); 27.5 g Fat; 4 g Protein; 172 mg Sodium

BAKED PIE SHELL: Roll out pastry. Turn 6 inch (15 cm) foil pie plate upside down. Cover with pastry on outside of pie plate. Prick all over with fork.

Trim edge. Bake in 400°F (205°C) oven for about 10 minutes to brown. Cool. Transfer to inside of 6 inch (15 cm) pie plate.

LEMON MERINGUE PIE

A most refreshing dessert.

Water	⅔ cup	150 mL
Granulated sugar	½ cup	125 mL
Cornstarch	2 tbsp.	30 mL
Lemon juice, fresh or bottled	3 tbsp.	50 mL
Egg yolk (large)	1	1
Water	2 tbsp.	30 mL
Pasty pie shell, page 114, 6 inch (15 cm), baked	1	1
MERINGUE		
Egg white (large), room temperature	1	1
Cream of tartar	⅛ tsp.	0.5 mL
Granulated sugar	2 tbsp.	30 mL

(continued on next page)

Heat first amount of water in saucepan until it boils.

Stir sugar and cornstarch together in small bowl. Add lemon juice, egg yolk and second amount of water. Mix well. Stir into boiling water until mixture returns to a boil and thickens.

Pour into pie shell.

Meringue: Beat egg white and cream of tartar together in small bowl until almost stiff. Gradually beat in sugar until stiff. Spoon over lemon filling, sealing to edge. Bake in 350°F (175°C) oven for about 10 minutes until golden brown. Cuts into 4 small wedges.

1 wedge contains: 264 Calories (1104 kJ); 8.2 g Fat; 3 g Protein; 71 mg Sodium

SPINACH FRUIT SALAD

Most attractive with a sweet and sour dressing.

Spinach leaves or romaine lettuce leaves	8-10	8-10
Pink grapefruit sections	6-8	6-8
Kiwifruit slices	6	6
Toasted sliced almonds	2 tsp.	10 mL
SWEET AND SOUR DRESSING		
White vinegar	1 tsp.	5 mL
Golden syrup	2 tbsp.	30 mL
Prepared mustard	1 tsp.	5 mL

Fold spinach leaves over using 4 or 5 per plate. Make a row just off center of plate, overlapping ends so as to make an unbroken sort of ridge. Place grapefruit sections in a row in front of leaves. Place kiwifruit slices in a row in front of grapefruit. Sprinkle almonds over fruit.

Sweet And Sour Dressing: Stir vinegar, syrup and mustard together in small bowl. Drizzle over spinach and fruit. Serves 2.

1 serving contains: 112 Calories (468 kJ); 1.5 g Fat; 2 g Protein; 58 mg Sodium

Pictured on front cover.

TOSSED SALAD

Greens with an added mixture of veggies and dressed with a doctored salad dressing.

Cut or torn head lettuce, lightly packed	1 cup	250 mL
Radishes, sliced	2-3	2-3
Green onion, sliced	1	1
Cherry tomatoes, diced	3-4	3-4
Process cheese slice, cut up (optional)	1	1
Salad dressing (or mayonnaise)	2 tbsp.	30 mL
Milk	1 tsp.	5 mL
Granulated sugar	¼ tsp.	1 mL

Place first 5 ingredients in bowl.

Stir salad dressing, milk and sugar together in small bowl. Shortly before serving, add to lettuce mixture. Toss. Serves 2.

1 serving contains: *89 Calories (373 kJ); 7.6 g Fat; 1 g Protein; 103 mg Sodium*

SALAD COMBO

Make this a day ahead. A combination of egg, vegetables and wine vinegar dressing.

Salad dressing (or mayonnaise)	¼ cup	60 mL
Red wine vinegar	1 tbsp.	15 mL
Frozen peas, cooked	1 cup	250 mL
Chopped celery	¼ cup	60 mL
Hard-boiled egg, chopped	1	1
Grated carrot	2 tbsp.	30 mL
Bean sprouts, small handful		
Dry onion flakes	2 tsp.	10 mL
Beef bouillon powder	1 tsp.	5 mL

Measure salad dressing and vinegar into medium bowl. Stir well.

Add remaining 7 ingredients. Toss to coat. Cover. Chill for 24 hours. Toss again before serving. Serves 2.

1 serving contains: *281 Calories (1178 kJ); 18.4 g Fat; 9 g Protein; 615 mg Sodium*

CUCUMBER IN SOUR CREAM

Dill adds greatly to the sour cream based marinade.

Small cucumber	**1**	**1**
Salt	**½ tsp.**	**2 mL**
Sour cream	**¼ cup**	**60 mL**
White vinegar	**1 tsp.**	**5 mL**
Chopped chives	**1 tsp.**	**5 mL**
Dill weed	**¼ tsp.**	**1 mL**
Pepper, sprinkle		

Score cucumber from top to bottom all down the outside edge with a fork. Slice thinly into bowl. Sprinkle with salt. Stir. Let stand for 30 to 45 minutes. Drain. Chill.

Stir next 5 ingredients together. Add to cucumber. Stir. Serves 2 generously.

1 serving contains: 64 Calories (269 kJ); 4.5 g Fat; 2 g Protein; 694 mg Sodium

MAKE-AHEAD SALAD

Make this a day ahead. Handy dry onion soup mix adds the flavor.

Frozen peas, cooked	**1 cup**	**250 mL**
Chopped celery	**¼ cup**	**60 mL**
Thinly sliced mild onion	**2 tbsp.**	**30 mL**
Hard-boiled egg, chopped	**1**	**1**
Grated cabbage, lightly packed	**¼ cup**	**60 mL**
Envelope dry onion soup mix **(stir well before measuring)**	**1 tbsp.**	**15 mL**
Red wine vinegar	**1 tbsp.**	**15 mL**
Salad dressing (or mayonnaise)	**2 tbsp.**	**30 mL**
Granulated sugar	**1 tsp.**	**5 mL**

Combine first 6 ingredients in bowl. Stir.

Mix vinegar, salad dressing and sugar in separate small bowl. Add to salad ingredients. Stir well. Cover and chill for 24 hours. Toss before serving. Serves 2.

1 serving contains: 193 Calories (807 kJ); 10.8 g Fat; 7 g Protein; 869 mg Sodium

CABBAGE SALAD

Colorful, so easy and quick. Simple to fix for one.

Shredded cabbage, lightly packed	1 cup	250 mL
Sliced celery	¼ cup	60 mL
Thinly sliced green onion	1 tsp.	5 mL
Slivered red pepper (or green)	1 tbsp.	15 mL
Grated carrot	1 tbsp.	15 mL
DRESSING		
Salad dressing (or mayonnaise)	2 tsp.	10 mL
Granulated sugar	2 tsp.	10 mL
White vinegar	2 tsp.	10 mL
Cooking oil	½ tsp.	2 mL
Milk	1½ tsp.	7 mL

Put first 5 ingredients into bowl.

Dressing: Measure all 5 ingredients into small cup. Stir together well. Add to salad. Toss. Makes 1 cup (250 mL). Serves 2.

1 serving contains: *66 Calories (275 kJ); 3.5 g Fat; 1 g Protein; 55 mg Sodium*

CHEESY PEA SALAD

A good variation of a green pea salad. Contains egg, cheese and green onion.

Frozen peas, cooked	1 cup	250 mL
Chopped celery	½ cup	125 mL
Hard-boiled egg, chopped	1	1
Diced medium or sharp Cheddar cheese	¼ cup	60 mL
Green onion, thinly sliced	½	½
Chopped pimiento	1 tsp.	5 mL
DRESSING		
Salad dressing (or mayonnaise)	2 tbsp.	30 mL
Milk	1½ tsp.	7 mL
Granulated sugar	¼ tsp.	1 mL
Salt, sprinkle		
Pepper, sprinkle		

(continued on next page)

Combine first 6 ingredients in bowl.

Dressing: Measure all 5 ingredients into small bowl. Stir together well. Pour over salad ingredients. Toss well. Serves 2.

1 serving contains: 224 Calories (936 kJ); 15.4 g Fat; 10 g Protein; 305 mg Sodium

OVERNIGHT COLESLAW

Might as well make lots. Can be kept for ages if left in its dressing.

Grated cabbage, lightly packed	**2 cups**	**500 mL**
Thinly sliced onion	**1/2 cup**	**125 mL**
Grated carrot	**1/4 cup**	**60 mL**
DRESSING		
White vinegar	**1/4 cup**	**60 mL**
Cooking oil	**1/4 cup**	**60 mL**
Granulated sugar	**1/4 cup**	**60 mL**
Celery seed	**1/4 tsp.**	**1 mL**
Dry mustard powder	**1/4 tsp.**	**1 mL**
Salt	**1/4 tsp.**	**1 mL**

Place cabbage, onion and carrot in bowl.

Dressing: Combine all 6 ingredients in small saucepan. Heat and stir until mixture comes to a boil. Pour immediately over cabbage mixture. Stir well. Cover. Chill in refrigerator overnight. Drain before serving or if not using all, remove with slotted spoon. Makes 1 1/2 cups (375 mL). Serves 2.

1 serving contains: 214 Calories (896 kJ); 14.2 g Fat; 2 g Protein; 197 mg Sodium

Pictured on page 143.

Paré Pointer

Are parasites what you see in Paris?

SEEDY SLAW

Full of seeds and sprouts.

Grated cabbage, lightly packed	1 cup	250 mL
Chopped green pepper	1½ tbsp.	25 mL
Sliced fresh mushrooms	¼ cup	60 mL
Bean sprouts, small handful		
Green onion, thinly sliced	1	1
DRESSING		
Ground walnuts or sunflower seeds	1½ tbsp.	25 mL
Toasted sesame seeds	1½ tbsp.	25 mL
Cooking oil	1½ tsp.	7 mL
White vinegar	1½ tsp.	7 mL
Granulated sugar	1 tsp.	5 mL
Dry mustard powder, just a pinch		
Water	1½ tsp.	7 mL
Worcestershire sauce	⅛ tsp.	0.5 mL
Chicken bouillon powder	¼ tsp.	1 mL
Salt	⅛ tsp.	0.5 mL
Pepper	1/16 tsp.	0.5 mL

Combine first 5 ingredients in medium bowl. Stir.

Dressing: Mix all 11 ingredients in small bowl. Stir well. Add to cabbage mixture. Toss. Make 1½ cups (375 mL). Serves 2.

1 serving contains: 136 Calories (571 kJ); 10.3 g Fat; 3 g Protein; 276 mg Sodium

TOMATO ASPIC

A little red jellied salad.

Unflavored gelatin	1½ tsp.	7 mL
Vegetable juice (such as V-8)	⅓ cup	75 mL
Onion powder	⅛ tsp.	0.5 mL
Salt, sprinkle		
Pepper, sprinkle		
Worcestershire sauce	⅛ tsp.	0.5 mL
Vegetable juice (such as V-8)	½ cup	125 mL
Diced celery	3 tbsp.	50 mL

(continued on next page)

Sprinkle gelatin over first amount of vegetable juice in small saucepan. Let stand for 1 minute. Heat and stir to dissolve gelatin.

Add onion powder, salt and pepper. Stir. Remove from heat.

Add Worcestershire sauce and second amount of vegetable juice. Chill until like thick syrup.

Stir in celery. Pour into 1 cup (250 mL) mold. Chill until firm. Makes 1 cup (250 mL). Serves 2.

1 serving contains: 30 Calories (127 kJ); trace Fat; 3 g Protein; 406 mg Sodium

SHRIMP ASPIC: Add about 10 cooked small shrimp just before pouring into the mold.

MACARONI SALAD

Really tasty. Contains egg, tomato and ham.

Elbow macaroni	1 cup	250 mL
Boiling water	1 qt.	1 L
Cooking oil (optional)	1 tsp.	5 mL
Salt (optional)	1 tsp.	5 mL
Hard-boiled egg, chopped	1	1
Medium tomato, halved, seeded and sliced	1	1
Thinly sliced or chopped celery	1/4 cup	60 mL
Cooked ham slices, cut in slivers	3	3
DRESSING		
Salad dressing (or mayonnaise)	1/4 cup	60 mL
Ketchup	1 tsp.	5 mL
Milk	2 tsp.	10 mL
Granulated sugar	1/2 tsp.	2 mL
Onion powder, just a pinch		
Chopped chives	1/2 tsp.	2 mL

Cook macaroni in boiling water, cooking oil and salt in large uncovered saucepan for 6 to 11 minutes until tender but firm. Drain. Rinse in cold water. Drain again. Turn into bowl.

Add egg, tomato, celery and ham. Stir.

Dressing: Measure all 6 ingredients into small bowl. Stir well. Pour over salad. Toss. Makes 4 cups (1 L).

1 cup (250 mL) contains: 260 Calories (1089 kJ); 12.4 g Fat; 10 g Protein; 493 mg Sodium

GREEN SALAD

Exceptionally easy to put together for one, two or more servings.

Shredded or chopped lettuce, lightly packed	1 cup	250 mL
Grated carrot	2 tbsp.	30 mL
Thinly sliced green onion	1 tsp.	5 mL
Slivered red or green pepper	1 tbsp.	15 mL
Sliced celery	¼ cup	60 mL
DRESSING		
Salad dressing (or mayonnaise)	4 tsp.	20 mL
White vinegar	2 tsp.	10 mL
Granulated sugar	2 tsp.	10 mL

Combine first 5 ingredients in bowl.

Dressing: Stir all 3 ingredients together well in small bowl. Pour over lettuce mixture. Toss. Makes 1 cup (250 mL).

1 serving contains: 154 Calories (642 kJ); 9.9 g Fat; 1 g Protein; 162 mg Sodium

WILTED SPINACH SALAD

A hot dressing stirred over spinach makes this a bit wilted. Excellent choice.

Cut or torn spinach or Romaine lettuce, lightly packed	2 cups	500 mL
White vinegar	4 tsp.	20 mL
Water	2 tsp.	10 mL
Green onion, sliced (or ⅛ tsp., 0.5 mL onion powder)	1	1
Bacon slice, cooked crisp then crumbled	1	1
Granulated sugar	1 tsp.	5 mL
Salt, sprinkle		
Pepper, sprinkle		
Hard-boiled egg, grated or finely chopped, for garnish	1	1

(continued on next page)

Place spinach in bowl.

Measure next 7 ingredients into small saucepan. Heat and stir until boiling. Pour over spinach. Stir well to wilt.

Sprinkle with grated egg. Serves 2.

1 serving contains: 80 Calories (335 kJ); 4.4 g Fat; 6 g Protein; 129 mg Sodium

POTATO SALAD

A moist salad that is easy to make in a small quantity.

Diced cooked potatoes	**1½ cups**	**375 mL**
Hard-boiled egg, chopped	**½**	**½**
Minced onion (or 1-2 green onions, chopped)	**2 tsp.**	**10 mL**
DRESSING		
Salad dressing (or mayonnaise)	**2 tbsp.**	**30 mL**
Commercial coleslaw dressing	**1½ tsp.**	**7 mL**
Prepared mustard	**⅛ tsp.**	**0.5 mL**
Milk	**1½ tsp.**	**7 mL**
Celery salt	**⅛ tsp.**	**0.5 mL**
Parsley flakes	**⅛ tsp.**	**0.5 mL**
Salt, sprinkle		
Pepper, sprinkle		
Hard-boiled egg, cut lengthwise in 4 wedges	**½**	**½**
Reserved dressing		
Paprika, sprinkle		

Put first 3 ingredients into bowl.

Dressing: Mix first 8 ingredients in small bowl. Reserve 2 tsp. (10 mL). Pour remaining dressing over potato mixture in bowl. Toss.

Garnish with egg wedges. Drizzle with reserved dressing. Sprinkle with paprika. Makes 1½ cups (375 mL). Serves 2.

1 serving contains: 241 Calories (1010 kJ); 12.3 g Fat; 6 g Protein; 333 mg Sodium

FRUIT SALAD

A tangy hot sauce is poured over the salad ingredients, cooling almost immediately.

Orange, peeled and segments cut up	1	1
Cherry tomatoes, sliced	2	2
Kiwifruit, peeled and sliced	1	1
Thinly sliced purple onion	½ cup	125 mL
DRESSING		
All-purpose flour	1½ tsp.	7 mL
Granulated sugar	2 tbsp.	30 mL
White vinegar	2 tbsp.	30 mL
Ketchup	1 tsp.	5 mL

Place orange, tomato, kiwifruit and onion in bowl. Toss.

Dressing: Stir flour and sugar together in small saucepan.

Stir in vinegar and ketchup. Heat and stir until mixture boils and thickens. Pour over salad ingredients. Toss. Makes 1¼ cups (300 mL). Serves 2.

1 serving contains: 138 Calories (577 kJ); trace Fat; 2 g Protein; 40 mg Sodium

Pictured on page 125.

1. Sausage Hors D'Oeuvres, page 11
2. Crab Gems, page 9
3. Oven Fried Chicken, page 98
4. Fruit Salad, page 124
5. Coconut Biscuits, page 20
6. Beefy Vegetable Soup, page 136

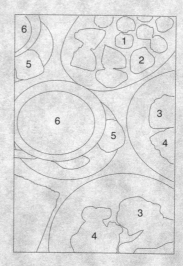

A mild flavor and so good.

Cooking oil	**2 tsp.**	**10 mL**
Small boneless, skinless chicken breast halves	**2**	**2**
Sliced celery	**¼ cup**	**60 mL**
Sliced almonds, toasted	**2 tbsp.**	**30 mL**
Crisp rice cereal	**¼ cup**	**60 mL**
Salad dressing (or mayonnaise)	**¼ cup**	**60 mL**
Lemon juice, fresh or bottled	**½ tsp.**	**2 mL**
Green onion, thinly sliced	**1**	**1**
Salt, sprinkle		
Pepper, just a pinch		

Heat cooking oil in frying pan. Add chicken. Fry, browning both sides, until no pink remains. Remove from heat. Cut into small pieces.

Place celery, almonds and rice cereal in bowl. Add chicken.

Combine salad dressing, lemon juice, green onion, salt and pepper in small bowl. Mix well. Add to chicken mixture. Stir. Turn into ungreased 1 quart (1 L) casserole. Bake, covered, in 400°F (205°C) oven for 15 to 20 minutes until heated through. Serves 2.

1 serving contains: 547 Calories (2290 kJ); 36 g Fat; 35 g Protein; 586 mg Sodium

Variation: To add a topping, mix 1 tbsp. (15 mL) melted butter or hard margarine with ¼ cup (60 mL) dry bread crumbs. Sprinkle over casserole. Bake, uncovered, in 400°F (205°C) oven for 15 to 20 minutes until heated through.

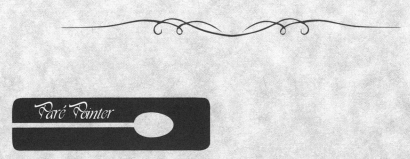

Paré Pointer

Comedians and surgeons have a lot in common. They are both cut-ups.

SEASONED DRESSING

A burnt orange color. A bit of a nip. Dress your greens with this.

Granulated sugar	1 tbsp.	15 mL
All-purpose flour	1 tsp.	5 mL
Seasoned salt	¼ tsp.	1 mL
White vinegar	2 tbsp.	30 mL
Water	2 tbsp.	30 mL
Cooking oil	1 tsp.	5 mL

Mix sugar, flour and salt well in small saucepan.

Add vinegar, water and cooking oil. Heat and stir until boiling and thickened slightly. Makes ¼ cup (60 mL).

2 tbsp. (30 mL) contain: *52 Calories (217 kJ); 2.3 g Fat; trace Protein; trace Sodium*

TANGY CAESAR SALAD

The red wine vinegar gives a different variation to this salad.

CAESAR DRESSING

Anchovy paste	1 tsp.	5 mL
Garlic powder	⅛ tsp.	0.5 mL
Worcestershire sauce	¼ tsp.	1 mL
Red wine vinegar	1 tsp.	5 mL
Cooking oil	1 tsp.	5 mL
Lemon juice, fresh or bottled	½ tsp.	2 mL
Grated Parmesan cheese	1 tbsp.	15 mL
Water	1 tbsp.	15 mL
Romaine lettuce, about ⅓ head, cut or torn		
Croutons	½ cup	125 mL

Grated Parmesan cheese (optional)

Caesar Dressing: Measure first 8 ingredients into medium bowl. Mix well.

Add lettuce and croutons. Toss.

Serve with additional Parmesan cheese to sprinkle over all. Serves 2.

1 serving contains: *91 Calories (381 kJ); 4 g Fat; 4 g Protein; 262 mg Sodium*

Pictured on page 17.

WHITE SAUCE

A basic sauce to use for many dishes such as vegetables, eggs, etc.

Butter or hard margarine	**1 tbsp.**	**15 mL**
All-purpose flour	**1 tbsp.**	**15 mL**
Salt	**$\frac{1}{4}$ tsp.**	**1 mL**
Pepper	**$\frac{1}{16}$ tsp.**	**0.5 mL**
Milk	**$\frac{1}{2}$ cup**	**125 mL**

Melt butter in small saucepan. Mix in flour, salt and pepper.

Stir or whisk in milk until mixture boils and thickens. Makes $\frac{1}{2}$ cup (125 mL).

2 tbsp. (30 mL) contain: 49 Calories (205 kJ); 3.6 g Fat; 1 g Protein; 215 mg Sodium

CHEESE SAUCE: Stir in $\frac{1}{4}$ cup (60 mL) grated medium or sharp Cheddar cheese until it melts. More cheese can be added if desired.

RAISIN SAUCE

Serve this good sauce with ham or pork.

Water	**$\frac{1}{4}$ cup**	**60 mL**
Cornstarch	**2 tsp.**	**10 mL**
Prepared orange juice	**$\frac{1}{4}$ cup**	**60 mL**
Brown sugar, packed	**1 tbsp.**	**15 mL**
Currant jelly preserves (or orange marmalade)	**2 tbsp.**	**30 mL**
Raisins	**2 tbsp.**	**30 mL**
Salt, just a pinch		

Combine all ingredients in saucepan. Heat and stir until mixture comes to a boil and thickens. May be cooled and reheated. Serve warm. Makes $\frac{1}{2}$ cup (125 mL).

2 tbsp. (30 mL) contain: 67 Calories (279 kJ); trace Fat; trace Protein; 3 mg Sodium

TARTAR SAUCE

Just a great partner for fish.

Salad dressing (or mayonnaise)	$1/4$ cup	60 mL
Finely chopped dill pickle	$1^1/_2$ tsp.	7 mL
Chopped chives	1 tsp.	5 mL
Tarragon	$1/_{16}$ tsp.	0.5 mL

Stir all 4 ingredients together. Chill until needed. Makes $1/4$ cup (60 mL).

1 tbsp. (15 mL) contains: *78 Calories (326kJ); 7.7 g Fat; trace Protein; 117 mg Sodium*

SAUCY HORSERADISH

Wonderful with roast beef.

Sour cream	$1/4$ cup	60 mL
Prepared horseradish	1 tbsp.	15 mL
Salt	$1/_8$ tsp.	0.5 mL

Mix all 3 ingredients in small bowl. Makes $1/4$ cup (60 mL).

1 tbsp. (15 mL) contains: *25 Calories (104 kJ); 2.2 g Fat; 1 g Protein; 98 mg Sodium*

FRENCH DRESSING

Dress any greens with this. You'll love it. Like the commercial variety.

Salad dressing (or mayonnaise)	$1/4$ cup	60 mL
Ketchup	$1^1/_2$ tsp.	7 mL
Lemon juice, fresh or bottled	2 tsp.	10 mL
Granulated sugar	$1/_2$ tsp.	2 mL
Prepared mustard	$1/4$ tsp.	1 mL
Seasoned salt	$1/4$ tsp.	1 mL

Measure all 6 ingredients into small bowl. Stir well. Makes $1/4$ cup (60 mL).

1 tbsp. (15 mL) contains: *82 Calories (345 kJ); 7.7 g Fat; trace Protein; 126 mg Sodium*

BROWN SUGAR SAUCE

Great for College Pudding, page 58 or to spoon over cake for dessert.

Brown sugar, packed	**¼ cup**	**60 mL**
All-purpose flour	**1 tbsp.**	**15 mL**
Salt	**⅛ tsp.**	**0.5 mL**
Water	**½ cup**	**125 mL**
Vanilla	**¼ tsp.**	**1 mL**
Butter or hard margarine (optional)	**1 tsp.**	**5 mL**

Combine sugar, flour and salt in saucepan. Mix well.

Stir in water and vanilla. Add butter. Heat and stir until mixture boils and thickens. Makes a generous ½ cup (125 mL).

2 tbsp. (30 mL) contain: 71 Calories (298 kJ); 1 g Fat; trace Protein; 103 mg Sodium

RUM SAUCE: Add ¼ tsp. (1 mL) rum flavoring.

CHOCOLATE SAUCE: Add 1¼ tsp. (6 mL) cocoa to sugar mixture.

BLENDER HOLLANDAISE SAUCE

Drizzle over asparagus or over steaks.

Egg yolk (large)	**1**	**1**
Lemon juice, fresh or bottled	**2 tsp.**	**10 mL**
Salt	**¹⁄₁₆ tsp.**	**0.5 mL**
Pepper, just a pinch		
Butter or hard margarine	**2 tbsp.**	**30 mL**

Place first 4 ingredients in blender. Do not process yet.

Melt butter in 1 cup (250 mL) liquid measure in microwave. Pour clarified (clear) butter into second small cup with pouring spout, discarding cloudy residue. Process ingredients in blender for about 3 seconds. Continue to process as you drizzle in clarified butter. Pour into cup. Cover. Let stand in warm water until needed. Makes 3 tbsp. (50 mL).

1 tbsp. (15 mL) contains: 89 Calories (374 kJ); 9.5 g Fat; 1 g Protein; 136 mg Sodium

CARAMEL SAUCE

Good over bananas, ice cream or make a sundae with your favorite nuts over top.

Butter or hard margarine	½ cup	125 mL
All-purpose flour	1½ tbsp.	25 mL
Brown sugar, packed	½ cup	125 mL
Granulated sugar	½ cup	125 mL
Dark corn syrup	1 tbsp.	15 mL
Skim evaporated milk (or light cream)	⅓ cup	75 mL
Vanilla	1 tsp.	5 mL

Melt butter in saucepan. Mix in flour.

Add remaining 5 ingredients. Boil until thick. Makes 1⅓ cups (325 mL).

2 tbsp. (30 mL) contain: *174 Calories (729 kJ); 9 g Fat; 1 g Protein; 105 mg Sodium*

BARBECUE SAUCE

This is incredible. A must try with ribs or pork chops. Keep any remaining sauce refrigerated.

Water	½ cup	125 mL
Cornstarch	3 tbsp.	50 mL
White vinegar	1 cup	250 mL
Brown sugar, packed	1 cup	250 mL
Ketchup	½ cup	125 mL
Mild molasses	¼ cup	60 mL
Worcestershire sauce	1 tsp.	5 mL
Dry mustard powder	½ tsp.	2 mL
Liquid smoke	½ tsp.	2 mL
Garlic powder	¼ tsp.	1 mL
Salt	¼ tsp.	1 mL

Stir water and cornstarch together in small saucepan.

Add remaining 9 ingredients. Heat and stir until mixture boils and thickens. Makes 3 cups (750 mL).

¼ cup (60 mL) contains: *114 Calories (475 kJ); 1 g Fat; trace Protein; 212 mg Sodium*

CAULIFLOWER SOUP

Smooth and white with green flakes showing. Good soup.

Water	1 cup	250 mL
Chopped cauliflower	2$\frac{1}{2}$ cups	625 mL
Chopped onion	$\frac{1}{3}$ cup	75 mL
Chicken bouillon powder	$\frac{1}{2}$ tsp.	2 mL
Salt	$\frac{1}{8}$ tsp.	0.5 mL
Pepper	$\frac{1}{16}$ tsp.	0.5 mL
Milk	1 cup	250 mL

Combine first 6 ingredients in saucepan. Cover. Cook for 10 to 12 minutes until tender. Do not drain.

Stir in milk. Pour into blender. Process until smooth. Return to saucepan. Heat through. Makes 3 cups (750 mL). Serves 2.

1 serving contains: 109 Calories (456 kJ); 2.9 g Fat; 7 g Protein; 429 mg Sodium

CAULIFLOWER CHEESE SOUP: Stir in 2 tbsp. (30 mL) grated sharp Cheddar cheese to melt or add to ingredients in blender.

ASPARAGUS SOUP

A smooth soup. Just the right consistency.

Water	1 cup	250 mL
Fresh asparagus, cut up	$\frac{1}{2}$ lb.	227 g
Butter or hard margarine	2 tbsp.	30 mL
All-purpose flour	2 tbsp.	30 mL
Salt	$\frac{1}{2}$ tsp.	2 mL
Pepper	$\frac{1}{8}$ tsp.	0.5 mL
Milk	2 cups	500 mL

Place water and asparagus in saucepan. Cook, covered, for about 10 minutes until tender. Do not drain. Pour into blender.

Melt butter in saucepan. Mix in flour, salt and pepper. Stir in milk until mixture boils and thickens. Add to blender. Purée. Return to saucepan to heat through. Makes 3$\frac{1}{4}$ cups (800 mL). Serves 2.

1 serving contains: 285 Calories (1193 kJ); 17 g Fat; 13 g Protein; 928 mg Sodium

CREAMY BROCCOLI SOUP

Smooth texture to this milky-green soup.

Fresh broccoli, cut up	2 cups	500 mL
Water	1 cup	250 mL
Reserved juice, plus water to make	1¼ cups	300 mL
Skim evaporated milk	1 cup	250 mL
Chicken bouillon powder	1 tsp.	5 mL
Salt	¼ tsp.	1 mL
Pepper	⅛-¼ tsp.	0.5-1 mL
All-purpose flour	2 tbsp.	30 mL

Cook broccoli in water in covered saucepan until tender. Drain and reserve juice. Put broccoli into blender.

Add remaining 6 ingredients to blender. Process until smooth. Return to saucepan. Heat, stirring occasionally, until mixture boils and thickens. Makes 3 cups (750 mL). Serves 2.

1 serving contains: 165 Calories (692 kJ); 1 g Fat; 14 g Protein; 845 mg Sodium

CHEESY BROCCOLI SOUP: Add ⅓ cup (75 mL) grated sharp Cheddar cheese to ingredients in blender. Process. More cheese may be added to taste.

CORN CHOWDER

Very tasty. The Parmesan adds a different flavor. For creative individual soup "bowls", hollow out small round bread loaves.

Diced potato	1 cup	250 mL
Sliced carrot	¼ cup	60 mL
Chopped onion	¼ cup	60 mL
Water	1 cup	250 mL
Celery salt, sprinkle		
Salt	½ tsp.	2 mL
Pepper	⅛ tsp.	0.5 mL
All-purpose flour	2 tbsp.	30 mL
Milk	1 cup	250 mL
Grated Parmesan cheese	¼ cup	60 mL
Cream style corn	1 cup	250 mL

(continued on next page)

Place first 7 ingredients in saucepan. Cover. Simmer for 15 to 20 minutes until tender.

Mix flour with part of milk until smooth. Add rest of milk. Stir into boiling vegetables until they return to a boil and thicken.

Add Parmesan cheese and corn. Stir. Heat through to melt cheese. Makes 3 cups (750 mL). Serves 2.

1 serving contains: 329 Calories (1378 kJ); 7.3 g Fat; 15 g Protein; 1387 mg Sodium

Pictured on page 143.

FISH CHOWDER

Cream-colored chowder. Pieces of celery, fish and potatoes all show.

Butter or hard margarine	1 tbsp.	15 mL
Chopped onion	$1/3$ cup	75 mL
Diced whitefish (such as cod or haddock)	1 cup	250 mL
Diced potato	1 cup	250 mL
Diced celery	$1/2$ cup	125 mL
Water	2 cups	500 mL
Salt	$3/4$ tsp.	4 mL
Pepper	$1/4$ tsp.	1 mL
Milk	2 cups	500 mL
All-purpose flour	$1/4$ cup	60 mL

Melt butter in large saucepan. Add onion. Sauté until onion is soft.

Add fish, potato and celery. Sauté 5 minutes.

Add water, salt and pepper. Boil slowly, covered, for 10 minutes.

Whisk milk into flour gradually in bowl until no lumps remain. Stir into boiling soup until mixture returns to a boil and thickens slightly. Makes 4 cups (1 L).

1 cup (250) contains: 205 Calories (857 kJ); 5.9 g Fat; 16 g Protein; 649 mg Sodium

BEEFY VEGETABLE SOUP

Beef and vegetables are in a dark flavorful broth.

Boneless beef, such as stew beef, diced	¼ lb.	113 g
Water	3 cups	750 mL
Chopped onion	½ cup	125 mL
Medium carrot, diced	1	1
Diced turnip	⅓ cup	75 mL
Small bay leaf	1	1
Parsley flakes	1/16 tsp.	0.5 mL
Ground rosemary or sage	1/16 tsp.	0.5 mL
Beef bouillon powder	1 tbsp.	15 mL
Pepper	1/16 tsp.	0.5 mL

Cook beef in water slowly in covered saucepan for 1 hour.

Add next 8 ingredients. Cover. Boil gently for about 30 minutes until vegetables are tender. Discard bay leaf. Makes a scant 4 cups (1 L).

1 cup (250 mL) contains: 54 Calories (225 kJ); 1.2 g Fat; 5 g Protein; 544 mg Sodium

Pictured on page 125.

CABBAGE VEGGIE SOUP

Colorful with the vegetables. Flavorful.

Medium potatoes, diced	1	1
Medium carrot, sliced	1	1
Chopped onion	½ cup	125 mL
Coarsely grated cabbage, lightly packed	1 cup	250 mL
Water	3 cups	750 mL
Chicken bouillon powder	1 tbsp.	15 mL
Salt, sprinkle		
Pepper, sprinkle		

Combine all 8 ingredients in saucepan. Cook, covered, for 15 to 20 minutes until vegetables are tender. Makes 3⅔ cups (900 mL). Serves 2.

1 serving contains: 103 Calories (430 kJ); 1 g Fat; 4 g Protein; 1163 mg Sodium

Cabbage always adds such a good flavor to soup. A full soup.

Boneless beef, such as stew beef, diced	1/4 lb.	113 g
Water	3 cups	750 mL
Chopped onion	1/4 cup	60 mL
Sliced carrot	1/4 cup	60 mL
Sliced celery	1/4 cup	60 mL
Diced turnip	1/4 cup	60 mL
Sliced small leek, white part only (optional)	1	1
Beef bouillon powder	1/4 tsp.	1 mL
Bay leaf	1/2	1/2
Ground thyme, just a pinch		
Parsley flakes	1/2 tsp.	2 mL
Ground cloves, just a pinch		
Salt	1/2 tsp.	2 mL
Pepper	1/8 tsp.	0.5 mL
Grated cabbage, lightly packed	1 cup	250 mL
French bread slices, dried, cut to fit (optional)	2	2

Combine beef and water in saucepan. Bring to a boil. Cover. Boil very slowly for 1 hour.

Add next 12 ingredients. Cook, covered, for 30 minutes.

Stir in cabbage. Cover and cook for 15 minutes.

Put bread slice in bottom of each of 2 soup bowls. Discard bay leaf. Divide soup between bowls. Makes 3 1/4 cups (800 mL). Serves 2.

1 serving contains: 86 Calories (361 kJ); 1.9 g Fat; 10 g Protein; 810 mg Sodium

Paré Pointer

At the end of an athlete's leg do you find athlete's foot?

CHICKEN SOUP

This homestyle soup is so colorful and inviting.

Water	2½ cups	625 mL
Boneless, skinless chicken breast half, diced	1	1
Finely diced (or sliced) carrot	¼ cup	60 mL
Thinly sliced celery	¼ cup	60 mL
Parsley flakes	½ tsp.	2 mL
Chicken bouillon powder	1 tsp.	5 mL
Salt	¼ tsp.	1 mL
Pepper	⅛ tsp.	0.5 mL
Spaghetti, broken in 1 inch (2.5 cm) pieces before measuring	¼ cup	60 mL

Measure first 8 ingredients into saucepan. Bring to a boil stirring often. Cover. Boil slowly for 30 minutes.

Add spaghetti. Cover. Continue to boil slowly for about 15 minutes until spaghetti is cooked. Makes 2¼ cups (550 mL). Serves 2.

1 serving contains: 132 Calories (552 kJ); 1.3 g Fat; 16 g Protein; 724 mg Sodium

CRAB SOUP

A really classy soup. Good with or without sherry. Cayenne can be halved or omitted if desired but it's great as is.

All-purpose flour	2 tbsp.	30 mL
Cayenne pepper	1/16 tsp.	0.5 mL
Salt	¼ tsp.	1 mL
Pepper	⅛ tsp.	0.5 mL
Skim evaporated milk	½ cup	125 mL
Milk	1½ cups	375 mL
Butter or hard margarine	1 tsp.	5 mL
Canned crabmeat, drained (or 1 cup, 250 mL fresh), membrane removed	4.2 oz.	120 g
Sherry (or alcohol-free sherry)	2 tbsp.	30 mL

(continued on next page)

Stir flour, cayenne, salt and pepper together in saucepan. Add first amount of milk gradually, whisking until no lumps remain.

Add remaining milk and butter. Heat and stir until boiling and thickened.

Stir in crabmeat and sherry. Heat through. Makes 2¼ cups (550 mL). Serves 2.

1 serving contains: 249 Calories (1041 kJ); 6.4 g Fat; 21 g Protein; 957 mg Sodium

ROYAL CREAM SQUARE

A cakey bottom with a cream cheese topping.

Large egg	1	1
Yellow cake mix, 1 layer size	½	½
Butter or hard margarine, softened	2 tbsp.	30 mL
Reserved ½ beaten egg		
Cream cheese, softened	4 oz.	125 g
Icing (confectioner's) sugar	¾ cup	175 mL
Reserved ½ beaten egg		
Vanilla	⅛ tsp.	0.5 mL
Icing (confectioner's) sugar, for dusting		

Beat egg in small bowl. Divide into 2 equal portions in custard cups or other small containers.

Combine cake mix, butter and ½ beaten egg in small bowl. Mix well. Press in greased 8 x 4 x 3 inch (20 x 10 x 7 cm) glass loaf pan. Bake in 325°F (160°C) oven for 15 minutes.

Beat cream cheese, icing sugar, second ½ beaten egg and vanilla together in separate bowl until fluffy. Spread over cake. Return to oven and bake for 20 to 22 minutes until set. Cool.

Dust with icing sugar. Cuts into 18 small squares.

1 square contains: 87 Calories (365 kJ); 4.8 g Fat; 1 g Protein; 63 mg Sodium

Variation: Strain 1 to 2 tbsp. (15 to 30 mL) apricot jam and drizzle over squares in place of icing sugar.

Pictured on page 53.

BROWNIES

Moist and not a very big panful. Double recipe for 8 x 8 inch (20 x 20 cm) pan.

Butter or hard margarine	¼ cup	60 mL
Unsweetened chocolate baking squares, cut up	1 oz.	28 g
Granulated sugar	½ cup	125 mL
Large egg	1	1
Vanilla	1 tsp.	5 mL
All-purpose flour	⅓ cup	75 mL
Salt, just a pinch		
Chopped walnuts (optional)	¼ cup	60 mL

Melt butter and chocolate in saucepan over medium-low heat, stirring often as it melts. Remove from heat.

Add sugar, egg and vanilla. Mix well.

Add flour, salt and walnuts. Stir. Turn into greased 8 x 4 x 3 inch (20 x 10 x 7 cm) glass loaf pan. Bake in 350°F (175°C) oven for about 20 minutes until an inserted wooden pick comes out clean but moist. Cuts into 18 squares.

1 square contains: 68 Calories (284 kJ); 3.6 g Fat; 1 g Protein; 31 mg Sodium

CHOCOLATE CHIP SQUARES

Moist and chewy.

Butter or hard margarine, softened	3 tbsp.	50 mL
Brown sugar, packed	⅔ cup	150 mL
Large egg	1	1
Vanilla	¼ tsp.	1 mL
All-purpose flour	⅔ cup	150 mL
Baking powder	½ tsp.	2 mL
Salt	⅛ tsp.	0.5 mL
Semisweet chocolate chips	½ cup	125 mL
Chopped walnuts or pecans (optional)	¼ cup	60 mL

(continued on next page)

Beat butter, sugar, egg and vanilla together in bowl.

Mix in flour, baking powder and salt.

Stir in chocolate chips and walnuts. Spread in greased 9 x 5 x 3 inch (22 x 12 x 7 cm) loaf pan. Bake in 350°F (175°C) oven for about 25 minutes. Cuts into 18 squares.

1 square contains: 92 Calories (386 kJ); 3.7 g Fat; 1 g Protein; 47 mg Sodium

OATMEAL CHIP SQUARES

A rich, sweet square. Rather coarse textured.

Butter or hard margarine	**2 tbsp.**	**30 mL**
Brown sugar, packed	**2 tbsp.**	**30 mL**
Maple syrup (or maple-flavored syrup)	**1 tbsp.**	**15 mL**
Quick cooking rolled oats (not instant)	**$3/4$ cup**	**175 mL**
All-purpose flour	**2 tbsp.**	**30 mL**
Baking powder	**$1/4$ tsp.**	**1 mL**
Large egg	**1**	**1**
ICING		
Semisweet chocolate chips	**2 tbsp.**	**30 mL**
Butterscotch chips	**2 tbsp.**	**30 mL**
Smooth peanut butter	**1 tbsp.**	**15 mL**

Melt butter in saucepan.

Stir in next 6 ingredients. Turn into greased $7^3/4$ x $3^3/4$ x $2^1/8$ inch (19.5 x 9.5 x 5.5 cm) foil loaf pan. Bake in 350°F (175°C) oven for about 20 minutes.

Icing: Melt both chips and peanut butter in saucepan over low heat stirring often. Smooth over squares. Cuts into 15 squares.

1 square contains: 70 Calories (291 kJ); 3.2 g Fat; 2 g Protein; 28 mg Sodium

Pictured on page 53.

CANDY BARS

These tiny squares disappear fast.

Butter or hard margarine, softened	**3 tbsp.**	**50 mL**
Brown sugar, packed	**3 tbsp.**	**50 mL**
Granulated sugar	**1 tbsp.**	**15 mL**
Smooth peanut butter	**1 tbsp.**	**15 mL**
Vanilla	**¼ tsp.**	**1 mL**
Rolled oats (not instant)	**¾ cup**	**175 mL**
ICING		
Semisweet chocolate chips	**¼ cup**	**60 mL**
Smooth peanut butter	**2 tbsp.**	**30 mL**

Beat first 5 ingredients together well in bowl.

Mix in rolled oats. Spread in greased 8 x 4 x 3 inch (20 x 10 x 7 cm) glass loaf pan. Bake in 375°F (190°C) oven for about 12 minutes.

Icing: Heat and stir chocolate chips and peanut butter in saucepan over medium-low heat. Spread over top. When set, this cuts into 18 squares or 6 good sized bars.

1 square contains: 69 Calories (288 kJ); 4.3 g Fat; 1 g Protein; 34 mg Sodium

1. Veggie Stir-Fry, page 150
2. Stuffed Potatoes, page 147
3. Overnight Coleslaw, page 119
4. Sauced Salmon, page 81
5. Corn Chowder, page 134

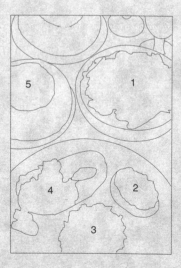

Wicker Mat Courtesy Of:
Wicker World

Glassware Courtesy Of:
Eaton's Housewares Dept.

Serving Dishes Courtesy Of:
Enchanted Kitchen

Rich and moist. Looks pretty on a plate.

BOTTOM LAYER

All-purpose flour	$\frac{1}{2}$ **cup**	**125 mL**
Brown sugar	**1 tbsp.**	**15 mL**
Butter or hard margarine, softened	$\frac{1}{4}$ **cup**	**60 mL**

TOP LAYER

Large egg	**1**	**1**
Brown sugar, packed	$\frac{2}{3}$ **cup**	**150 mL**
Vanilla	$\frac{1}{2}$ **tsp.**	**2 mL**
Salt	$\frac{1}{8}$ **tsp.**	**0.5 mL**
Chopped walnuts or pecans (optional)	$\frac{1}{4}$ **cup**	**60 mL**
Rolled oats (not instant)	$\frac{1}{4}$ **cup**	**60 mL**

Bottom Layer: Mix all 3 ingredients in bowl until crumbly. Pack in greased 8 x 4 x 3 inch (20 x 10 x 7 cm) glass loaf pan. Bake in 350°F (175°C) oven for 12 minutes.

Top Layer: Beat egg well in bowl. Add brown sugar, vanilla and salt. Beat.

Stir in walnuts and rolled oats. Smooth over bottom layer. Bake in 350°F (175°C) oven for 20 minutes. Cuts into 18 squares.

1 square contains: 81 Calories (340 kJ); 3.1g Fat; 1 g Protein, 54 mg Sodium

Pictured on page 53.

A tattletale pig will always squeal on you.

PECAN CHEWS

Nutty and chewy. Ice with Butter Icing, page 30, if desired.

Butter or hard margarine, softened	¹/₄ cup	60 mL
Brown sugar, packed	¹/₂ cup	125 mL
Granulated sugar	2 tbsp.	30 mL
Large egg	1	1
Vanilla	¹/₂ tsp.	2 mL
All-purpose flour	²/₃ cup	150 mL
Salt	¹/₈ tsp.	0.5 mL
Chopped pecans	¹/₄ cup	60 mL

Measure first 5 ingredients into bowl. Beat well.

Stir in remaining 3 ingredients. Turn into greased 8 x 4 x 3 inch (20 x 10 x 7 cm) glass loaf pan. Bake in 350°F (175°C) oven for 20 to 25 minutes. Cuts into 18 squares.

1 square contains: 87 Calories (365 kJ); 4.2 g Fat; 1 g Protein; 53 mg Sodium

ONION AND APPLE

An excellent dish to serve with pork.

Butter or hard margarine	1 tbsp.	15 mL
Sliced onion	1 cup	250 mL
Peeled and sliced cooking apple (McIntosh is good)	1 cup	250 mL
Granulated sugar	1¹/₂ tsp.	7 mL
Salt	¹/₄ tsp.	1 mL

Melt margarine in frying pan. Add onion. Sauté until soft.

Add apple, sugar and salt. Stir. Cover. Lower heat. Barely simmer for 4 to 5 minutes until apple is soft. Serves 2.

1 serving contains: 119 Calories (497 kJ); 6.1 g Fat; 1 g Protein; 400 mg Sodium

Serve these already dressed for the table.

Medium potatoes	2	2
Creamed cottage cheese	¼ cup	60 mL
Green onion, sliced	1	1
Skim milk (or other)	2 tbsp.	30 mL
Onion powder	¹⁄₁₆ tsp.	0.5 mL
Salt	⅛ tsp.	0.5 mL
Pepper, sprinkle		

Grated medium or sharp Cheddar cheese, sprinkle

Paprika, sprinkle, for garnish
Chopped chives, for garnish

Pierce potatoes in 5 or 6 places each. Bake in 400°F (205°C) oven for about 45 minutes until tender when pierced with paring knife. Cool until you can handle. Cut thin layer off top lengthwise. Scoop out potato into bowl leaving shells at least ¼ inch (6 mm) thick.

Add next 6 ingredients. Mash together well. Stuff shells.

Sprinkle with cheese. Return to oven. Bake for 15 to 20 minutes until hot.

Sprinkle with paprika and chives. Serves 2.

1 serving contains: 253 Calories (1061 kJ); 1 g Fat; 9 g Protein; 323 mg Sodium

Pictured on page 143.

BASIC RICE

Fast and easy.

Long grain rice (see Note)	½ cup	125 mL
Water	1 cup	250 mL
Salt	¼ tsp.	1 mL

Combine all 3 ingredients in small saucepan. Bring to a boil. Boil slowly, covered, for about 15 minutes until rice is tender and water is absorbed. Fluff with fork. Makes 1⅓ cups (325 mL).

⅔ cup (150 mL) contains: 178 Calories (746 kJ); trace Fat; 3 g Protein; 342 mg Sodium

Note: If you wish to prepare larger servings, use ⅔ cup (150 mL) rice and 1⅓ cups (300 mL) water. Makes 2 cups (500 mL).

MILD CURRIED CORN

Most unusual but most pleasant. Amount of curry can be varied to taste.

Hard margarine (butter browns too fast)	1 tbsp.	15 mL
Kernel corn, fresh or frozen	1 cup	250 mL
Diced onion	1 tbsp.	15 mL
Diced green pepper	1 tbsp.	15 mL
Curry powder	¼ tsp.	1 mL
Granulated sugar, just a pinch		
Sour cream	3 tbsp.	50 mL
Salt, sprinkle		
Pepper, sprinkle		

Melt margarine in saucepan. Add corn, onion, green pepper and curry powder. Sauté until tender.

Add remaining 4 ingredients. Heat and stir until hot. Serves 2.

1 serving contains: *157 Calories (659 kJ); 8.8 g Fat; 3 g Protein; 80 mg Sodium*

PARSNIPS AND ORANGE

Nicely glazed. Extra tasty.

Parsnips, cut up (½ lb., 227 g)	1½ cups	375 mL
Boiling water, 1 inch (2.5 cm) deep		
Salt	¼ tsp.	1 mL
Prepared orange juice	4 tsp.	20 mL
Brown sugar	1½ tbsp.	25 mL
Butter or hard margarine	2 tsp.	10 mL
Lemon juice, fresh or bottled	¼ tsp.	1 mL

Cook parsnips in boiling water and salt until tender. Drain.

Stir orange juice, brown sugar, butter and lemon juice together in small bowl. Add to parsnips. Shake pan well to distribute, stirring and tossing as needed. Serves 2.

1 serving contains: *162 Calories (676 kJ); 4.2 g Fat; 1 g Protein; 54 mg Sodium*

GREEN BEAN CASSEROLE

Soy sauce adds to the flavor of this dish. Also makes it a darker color.

Condensed cream of mushroom soup	1/2 x 10 oz.	1/2 x 284 mL
Soy sauce	1 tsp.	5 mL
Canned green beans, drained (or frozen, cooked and drained)	10 oz.	284 mL
Grated medium or sharp Cheddar cheese (optional)	2 tbsp.	30 mL
Slivered almonds (optional)	2 tbsp.	30 mL

Stir soup and soy sauce together in small bowl. Add beans. Stir. Turn into ungreased 1 quart (1 L) casserole.

Sprinkle with cheese and almonds. Bake, uncovered, in a 350°F (175°C) oven for 25 to 30 minutes. Serves 2.

1 serving contains: 98 Calories (408 kJ); 5.8 g Fat; 2.5 g Protein; 1010 mg Sodium

SAUTÉED PEAS

Onion gives the peas an extra lift.

Hard margarine	2 tsp.	10 mL
Thinly sliced onion	1/2 cup	125 mL
Frozen peas	1 cup	250 mL
Salt, sprinkle		
Pepper, sprinkle		

Melt margarine in saucepan. Add onion. Sauté until soft.

Add peas. Sprinkle with salt and pepper. Stir. Cover. Simmer very slowly, stirring occasionally, for about 5 minutes to cook peas. Serves 2.

1 serving contains: 111 Calories (463 kJ); 4 g Fat; 5 g Protein; 118 mg Sodium

VEGGIE STIR-FRY

You're in luck when you can buy vegetables in small quantities. Makes this a cinch.

Thinly sliced carrot	¼ cup	60 mL
Chopped onion	¼ cup	60 mL
Water	½ cup	125 mL
Broccoli florets	½ cup	125 mL
Cauliflower florets	¼ cup	60 mL
Zucchini slivers with peel	¼ cup	60 mL
Snow peas, fresh or frozen, thawed	¼ cup	60 mL
Cherry tomatoes, quartered	2	2
Tiny whole fresh mushrooms	¼ cup	60 mL
or large, sliced		
Cornstarch	¾ tsp.	4 mL
Water	1 tsp.	5 mL
Skim evaporated milk	¼ cup	60 mL
Seasoned salt	¼ tsp.	1 mL
Salt, sprinkle		
Pepper, sprinkle		

Place carrot, onion and water in non-stick wok or frying pan. Cover. Simmer for 5 minutes. Remove cover.

Add broccoli, cauliflower, zucchini and snow peas. Stir-fry until cooked tender-crisp.

Add tomatoes and mushrooms. Stir-fry for 2 minutes.

Stir cornstarch into water. Mix into milk. Add seasoned salt. Stir into vegetable mixture until bubbling and thickened. Sprinkle with salt and pepper. Serves 2.

1 serving contains: *72 Calories (303 kJ); trace Fat; 5 g Protein; 57 mg Sodium*

Pictured on page 143.

Paré Pointer

Astronomy is a science that is over your head

Throughout this book measurements are given in Conventional and Metric measure. To compensate for differences between the two measurements due to rounding, a full metric measure is not always used. The cup used is the standard 8 fluid ounce. Temperature is given in degrees Fahrenheit and Celsius. Baking pan measurements are in inches and centimetres as well as quarts and litres. An exact metric conversion is given below as well as the working equivalent (Standard Measure).

OVEN TEMPERATURES

Fahrenheit (°F)	Celsius (°C)
175°	80°
200°	95°
225°	110°
250°	120°
275°	140°
300°	150°
325°	160°
350°	175°
375°	190°
400°	205°
425°	220°
450°	230°
475°	240°
500°	260°

SPOONS

Conventional Measure	Metric Exact Conversion Millilitre (mL)	Metric Standard Measure Millilitre (mL)
$1/8$ teaspoon (tsp.)	0.6 mL	0.5 mL
$1/4$ teaspoon (tsp.)	1.2 mL	1 mL
$1/2$ teaspoon (tsp.)	2.4 mL	2 mL
1 teaspoon (tsp.)	4.7 mL	5 mL
2 teaspoons (tsp.)	9.4 mL	10 mL
1 tablespoon (tbsp.)	14.2 mL	15 mL

CUPS

$1/4$ cup (4 tbsp.)	56.8 mL	60 mL
$1/3$ cup ($5^{1}/3$ tbsp.)	75.6 mL	75 mL
$1/2$ cup (8 tbsp.)	113.7 mL	125 mL
$2/3$ cup ($10^{2}/3$ tbsp.)	151.2 mL	150 mL
$3/4$ cup (12 tbsp.)	170.5 mL	175 mL
1 cup (16 tbsp.)	227.3 mL	250 mL
$4^{1}/2$ cups	1022.9 mL	1000 mL (1 L)

PANS

Conventional Inches	Metric Centimetres
8x8 inch	20x20 cm
9x9 inch	22x22 cm
9x13 inch	22x33 cm
10x15 inch	25x38 cm
11x17 inch	28x43 cm
8x2 inch round	20x5 cm
9x2 inch round	22x5 cm
10x$4^{1}/2$ inch tube	25x11 cm
8x4x3 inch loaf	20x10x7.5 cm
9x5x3 inch loaf	22x12.5x7.5 cm

DRY MEASUREMENTS

Conventional Measure Ounces (oz.)	Metric Exact Conversion Grams (g)	Metric Standard Measure Grams (g)
1 oz.	28.3 g	28 g
2 oz.	56.7 g	57 g
3 oz.	85.0 g	85 g
4 oz.	113.4 g	125 g
5 oz.	141.7 g	140 g
6 oz.	170.1 g	170 g
7 oz.	198.4 g	200 g
8 oz.	226.8 g	250 g
16 oz.	453.6 g	500 g
32 oz.	907.2 g	1000 g (1 kg)

CASSEROLES (Canada & Britain)

Standard Size Casserole	Exact Metric Measure
1 qt. (5 cups)	1.13 L
$1^{1}/2$ qts. ($7^{1}/2$ cups)	1.69 L
2 qts. (10 cups)	2.25 L
$2^{1}/2$ qts. ($12^{1}/2$ cups)	2.81 L
3 qts. (15 cups)	3.38 L
4 qts. (20 cups)	4.5 L
5 qts. (25 cups)	5.63 L

CASSEROLES (United States)

Standard Size Casserole	Exact Metric Measure
1 qt. (4 cups)	900 mL
$1^{1}/2$ qts. (6 cups)	1.35 L
2 qts. (8 cups)	1.8 L
$2^{1}/2$ qts. (10 cups)	2.25 L
3 qts. (12 cups)	2.7 L
4 qts. (16 cups)	3.6 L
5 qts. (20 cups)	4.5 L

INDEX

Company's Coming cookbooks are available at retail locations throughout Canada!

EXCLUSIVE mail order offer on next page

Buy any 2 cookbooks—choose a 3rd FREE of equal or less value than the lowest price paid.

Original Series   CA$15.99 Canada   US$12.99 USA & International

CODE		CODE		CODE	
SQ	150 Delicious Squares	BB	Breakfasts & Brunches	ASI	Asian Cooking
CA	Casseroles	SC	Slow Cooker Recipes	CB	The Cheese Book
MU	Muffins & More	ODM	One-Dish Meals	RC	The Rookie Cook
SA	Salads	ST	Starters	RHR	Rush-Hour Recipes
AP	Appetizers	SF	Stir-Fry	SW	Sweet Cravings
SS	Soups & Sandwiches	MAM	Make-Ahead Meals	YRG	Year-Round Grilling
CO	Cookies	PB	The Potato Book	GG	Garden Greens
PA	Pasta	CCLFC	Low-Fat Cooking	CHC	Chinese Cooking
BA	Barbecues	CCLFP	Low-Fat Pasta	PK	The Pork Book
PR	Preserves	CFK	Cook For Kids	RL	Recipes for Leftovers
CH	Chicken, Etc.	SCH	Stews, Chilies & Chowders		
KC	Kids Cooking	FD	Fondues		
CT	Cooking For Two	CCBE	The Beef Book		

Greatest Hits Series

CODE	CA$12.99 Canada US$9.99 USA & International
ITAL	Italian
MEX	Mexican

Lifestyle Series

CODE	CA$17.99 Canada US$15.99 USA & International
GR	Grilling
DC	Diabetic Cooking

CODE	CA$19.99 Canada US$15.99 USA & International
HC	Heart-Friendly Cooking
DDI	Diabetic Dinners **NEW** *March 1/04*

Most Loved Recipe Collection

CODE	CA$23.99 Canada US$19.99 USA & International
MLA	Most Loved Appetizers
MLMC	Most Loved Main Courses **NEW** *April 1/04*

Special Occasion Series

CODE	CA$20.99 Canada US$19.99 USA & International
GFK	Gifts from the Kitchen
CFS	Cooking for the Seasons

CODE	CA$22.99 Canada US$19.99 USA & International
WC	Weekend Cooking

CODE	CA$25.99 Canada US$22.99 USA & International
HFH	Home for the Holidays
DD	Decadent Desserts

Company's Coming COOKBOOKS®

Company's Coming Publishing Limited
2311 – 96 Street
Edmonton, Alberta, Canada T6N 1G3
Tel: 780-450-6223 Fax: 780-450-1857
www.companyscoming.com

EXCLUSIVE Mail Order Offer

See previous page for list of cookbooks

Buy 2 Get 1 FREE!

Buy any 2 cookbooks—choose a **3rd FREE** of equal or less value than the lowest price paid.

Quantity	Code	Title	Price Each	Price Total
			$	$
		DON'T FORGET to indicate your FREE BOOK(S). (see exclusive mail order offer above) please print		
	TOTAL BOOKS (including FREE)	**TOTAL BOOKS PURCHASED:**	$	

	International	Canada & USA
Plus Shipping & Handling (per destination)	$11.98 (one book)	$5.98 (one book)
Additional Books (including FREE books)	$ ($4.99 each)	$ ($1.99 each)
Sub-Total	$	$
Canadian residents add G.S.T.(7%)		$
TOTAL AMOUNT ENCLOSED	$	$

The Fine Print

- Orders outside Canada must be **PAID IN US FUNDS** by cheque or money order drawn on Canadian or US bank or by credit card.
- Make cheque or money order payable to: **Company's Coming Publishing Limited.**
- Prices are expressed in Canadian dollars for Canada, US dollars for USA & International and are subject to change without prior notice.
- Orders are shipped surface mail. For courier rates, visit our web-site: **www.companyscoming.com** or contact us: **Tel: 780-450-6223 Fax: 780-450-1857.**
- Sorry, no C.O.D.'s.

☐ MasterCard ☐ VISA

_____ Expiry date

Account # _____

Name of cardholder _____

Cardholder's signature _____

Gift Giving

- Let us help you with your gift giving!
- We will send cookbooks directly to the recipients of your choice if you give us their names and addresses.
- Please specify the titles you wish to send to each person.
- If you would like to include your personal note or card, we will be pleased to enclose it with your gift order.
- Company's Coming Cookbooks make excellent gifts: Birthdays, bridal showers, Mother's Day, Father's Day, graduation or any occasion ...collect them all!

Shipping Address

Send the cookbooks listed above to:

Name: _____

Street: _____

City: _____ Prov./State: _____

Country: _____ Postal Code/Zip: _____

Tel: (_____) _____

Email address: _____

☐ YES! Please send a catalogue _____